T0064545

THE COMPLETE
GOLFER

REACHING YOUR ULTIMATE
GOLF POTENTIAL

PAUL MEYER

Golf Methodologist and Strategist
Teaching Professional
Tampa, FL

authorHOUSE®

AuthorHouse™
1663 Liberty Drive
Bloomington, IN 47403
www.authorhouse.com
Phone: 1 (800) 839-8640

Published by AuthorHouse: 08/28/2015

ISBN: 978-1-5049-2769-7 (sc)
ISBN: 978-1-5049-2768-0 (e)

Print information available on the last page.

This book is printed on acid-free paper.

CONTENTS

FOREWORD

As a parent of a young boy, I realized In Paul's early life what a positive influence the game of golf had on his attitude and outlook on life. It became apparent that this was an activity that allowed him the opportunity to set goals, establish a consistent work/practice ethic and strive for proficiency. These traits apply not only to golf but to all of Paul's other lifetime endeavors. Through the game of golf he has had to practice the art of patience, monitor his attitude, and accept the axiom: As in life, one must take the good golf days with the bad.

DeWayne Meyer

FOREWORD

I first met Paul Meyer when I was in 8th grade and "Coach" asked me to come see him in his classroom. He was the new High School boys golf coach and he asked me to sign up for his junior golf clinics over the summer. Coach heard about my talent and wanted to start working with me as soon as possible. Nearly 2 decades later, he is still my coach, close friend, and mentor.

Teaming up with Coach has brought my game to levels that I only dreamed of back in 8th grade. I have found success at every level of competition, earning All-State honors in High School and All-American honors in College. I've qualified for several USGA events and was the Wisconsin Amateur Player of the Year in my final year as an amateur. As a professional, I have 11 career wins and am currently a member of WEB.COM Tour. My consistent improvement year after year was the result of hard work with Coach on the course, range, and even on the telephone.

Paul Meyer has experiences from every aspect of life and his vast intelligence combined with an endless passion for the game of golf makes him perfectly qualified to write a book on the subject. Coach has experienced golf from the side of a player, student, coach, and teacher. More importantly, he has 20+ years experience as an educator, which has given him an indecipherable ability to read golfers for the individuals they are. Reading "The Complete Golfer" will give golfers a unique look at how Paul Meyer has developed so many golfers into champions. He will teach you to find your individual swing and avoid the traps of cookie-cutter instruction.

PAUL MEYER

I have spent a majority of the last 5 years on the road traveling between tournaments, but I have considered myself extremely lucky to have Paul as my coach. He took whatever talent I had and developed it into the skills I have today as a playing professional. I can't wait to see what another couple of decades with Paul at my side will lead to.

Neil Johnson
Web.com/ PGA Canada

COACH

Coach Paul Meyer has played a big role in my life and the development of my golf game since I was 9 years old. I call him coach because he doesn't just instruct my swing. He teaches all aspects of the game; shaping and influencing the player to be strong in all areas of the game.

My name is Garrett Loomis. I am a senior at River Falls High School in River Falls, WI. Over the past 8 years Paul has taught me how to not just play the game of golf, but how to play the game of golf well and with a high level of character and integrity. I first met coach on the River Falls Golf Club driving range the spring of 2006. At the time, Paul had a great reputation around the state as a top High School coach in Wisconsin. He coached River Falls to 3 state titles and multiple individual state champions in the matter of 7 years. Paul retired from coaching in 2007. Knowing this, my parents knew who to get me started with. As a young player he focused on teaching me the rules of the game and the fundamentals of the golf swing. The first couple of years he taught in terms I could relate to. I played baseball, and many times in the first couple of years he would relate what we were working on to baseball. For example, the take-away was one of the first things we started working on, he instructed me to bring the club right back into the catcher's mitt. It allowed me to understand the concept and refine it much more efficient. At a young age he noticed I hit the ball farther than most kids and had a lot of potential. He never tried to take my power away from me, instead he taught me how to control it, when to use it and when not to. He really encouraged me from the start comparing me to other good players he has coached, mentioning I had the most natural swing he has ever seen. Had he not said these things, I'm not sure I would work as hard as I do to become the best I can. Paul took me under his wing and made it a mission to see me through to wherever I might end up in the future.

Being an 8th grade American History teacher at Meyer Middle School in River Falls, WI, Mr. Meyer and I gave each other plenty of grief. It was fun to hop into the car with him after school and head to the course for our after-school lesson. Something I'm sure we both looked forward to everyday. We did this all throughout middle school. This is the stage in my career where I grew the most as a golfer and started developing the game and swing I would have for the rest of my life. In 6th grade he asked me what my goals were. I told him I wanted to be on varsity as a freshman but that was pretty much it. I never really heard of goals at the time, so we discussed some goals I should have all the way trough the time I graduate. He agreed with making varsity as a freshman, but told me my potential suggested bigger things. I should have the goal of being a WIAA State Champion, winning big summer tournaments in Wisconsin and the Midwest and playing Division I college golf.

I went home and wrote the goals down in a piece of paper and hung it on my bathroom mirror as he suggested. This past August I won the WSGA State Junior, achieving one of my goals. In addition to that I signed my National Letter of Intent with Marquette University this November, achieving another one of the original goals. Paul embedded the idea into me that golf is a process; all great things take time. Since then I have lengthened my list of goals and made them more specific. Paul has always been a mentor and someone to talk to. The night before big or very meaningful tournaments I often text or call Paul. He tells me what I need to hear by motivating me and helping me calm down in addition to reminding me that golf is just a game.

In my years at River Falls High School Paul handed off the role of being a swing coach to my High School coach Matt Garber. A good friend of his that he played college golf with. I still wanted him to be involved with my game so he agreed to help me in any way he could. Paul then took up the role of more of a mental coach and someone to play with and discuss course management. In addition to that, he played a huge role in my communication with colleges, helping me get interest and giving me ideas on what programs might be a good fit for me. Coach made any phone call he could to help me in the process. He has seen me grow as a player and person since I was in fourth grade.

Most of all Paul and I have created a friendship. It is a friendship that I will be thankful for having for the rest of my life. He has taught me so many things along the way and I look forward to learning much more. Although I know I will soon become busier due to me leaving for college next fall and a more competitive summer schedule, I look forward to spending my future summers playing and practicing with him on the courses where our relationship started.

Garrett Loomis
Marquette University

ACKNOWLEDGEMENTS

I would like to thank many people for supporting me in my golf endeavors. First, I would like to thank Deb for supporting my passion and joy for this great game. Second, I would like to thank my father, DeWayne, for introducing me to the game at an early age and showing me that golf truly is a lifetime sport. Third, I want to thank my mother, Sue, for allowing me to be gone all day ; every day during the summer months when I was young. I would also like to thank Dave Cronk, my high school golf coach and friend for holding me to the line and continuing to be a respected member of my golf life. I want to also acknowledge my former teammates in high school and college for instilling in me a competitive drive, my former high school players who demanded my time and efforts as their high school coach, and my current golf students who trust me to help them with this great game of golf.

I would like to give a special thanks to my colleague, Stephanie Reid, for proofreading and editing my copy and to Judy Langford for her excellent comments on format and presentation.

Lastly, I would like to thank PGA Professional, Rick Bradshaw, for countless hours of talking golf, redefining golf for me at 49 years old, for introducing me to Percy Boomer Theory, and for being a great friend and mentor in my relocation to Florida.

I would like to dedicate this work to my
children; Kayla, Jake, and Tannah

INTRODUCTION

Welcome to the "Complete Golfer" manual written for you to reach your true golfing potential. I have envisioned doing a user friendly workbook for many years. Now that I have retired from my duties as a golf coach at River Falls High School and have adapted to the beautiful Florida climate I have worked hard in developing my professional teaching methodology. I can now pursue a new avenue in my golfing life both as a player and instructor. I have accomplished many things as a coach, teacher, mentor, and player. I have played golf since I was 8 years old. I played on my high school team and for the University of Wisconsin-Eau Claire. I now play professionally in local and state events and someday I hope to be able to take it nationally. I hope that the knowledge I have gained will help you accomplish what you want out of your golfing life.

If you ask most of the people who know me, they would tell you that I'm devoted to the entire concept of golf. Whether it is equipment, clothing, shoes, balls, literature, DVD, internet, swing thought theory, mental conditioning or trying to guess who a player is by watching their swing before they flash the name on TV, I'm in! WEB.COM, NCAA, PGA, LPGA, Asian, European tours - if it is on TV, I have it on. My DVR is loaded with all the Golf Channel instruction shows and my computer has hundreds of clips and links related to golf. It is not a hobby, it is my professional life. I'm a golf junkie and proud of it. I love this game and I want to share what I've learned with the multitudes of golfers who want to improve.

Although my original thought was to design this manual for high school coaches and golfers, it will be very useful for any golfer. This manual can be used as a guide for setting up a variety of clinics, programs, and seminars as well as develop the skills of the individual golfer. Through my own research and practice, I've developed my own philosophy on becoming a "Complete Golfer". My drills and routines will help you improve in your physical and mental preparation for golf. Although I have my theories, my 24 years as a middle school teacher allow me to teach in a manner that is relevant to the individual. It is not a "One size fits all" theory. It is imperative to take into account each individual's strengths and weaknesses and design lessons and practice drills geared to them and what they want to accomplish in golf.

My goal in my camps, seminars and this manual is to give you a new mental and physical outlook at golf combined with giving you the background, knowledge, processes, and routines that are needed to conduct motivated, focused, quality practice sessions that can be transferred to the golf course. I want to help you in your journey to become a successful competitor against the course, your opponent and yourself. This manual will help you become the "Complete Golfer" you want to be. It focuses on the tangible areas of golf (range, course, scoring zone) and the intangible areas (mental, emotional, strategy, fear, and tension). This manual describes a problem and then attempts to describe a solution.

I've enjoyed writing this manual and I hope you find it enjoyable and useful. I wish you the best of luck in becoming a "Complete Golfer".

Paul Meyer
Teaching Professional

MISSION STATEMENT

My mission in "The Complete Golfer" is to provide a practical and useful resource book for coaches, parents, and teachers involved in junior golf and team competition that will enhance their coaching and strengthen their golf program. Furthermore, this manual will allow golfers of every ability and interest level the necessary strategies to improve their mental and physical components to tap into their true golf potential.

MENTAL GOLF

How do we prepare and use our mind to play better golf?

THE COMPLETE GOLFER

PHASE ONE: DEVELOPING YOUR MENTAL GAME

Develop a system that allows the proper mental framework, routines, and habits that build confidence and belief in you!

In this section you will learn about the following areas:

- Goal Setting
- Practice Mode vs. Playing Mode
- Individual Shot Analysis (pre-shot, performance, post-shot)
- Positive Self Talk and Mantras
  - Think it, Say it, Do it
- Reducing Tension and Overcoming Fear
- Lowering Your Comfort Zone
- Establishing Methods to Score Lower

LEARNING

Before we begin this journey to becoming a "Complete Golfer" I want you to consider what type of learner you are. I think there are three methods of learning that apply to golf:

Auditory- you learn by listening

Visual- you learn by watching, reading, seeing

Kinesthetic- you learn by doing and practicing

The easy question is: Don't you have to be all three? The easy answer is: Yes! Each of us has strengths in how we learn. I am a Visual-Kinesthetic learner. I need to see it and then do it. That is the case with most of my students. I lose them when I talk too much theory. I get them back when I show them or put them in a certain golf position. The more senses you can involve in the learning process the quicker you will be able to remember it and do it. Find out how you learn and find an instructor that will cater to your style!

THE GOLF SPECTRUM

Here is another point to consider: What type of golfer are you? What type of golfer do you want to become? Just like people vary on the political spectrum, so to, do they vary on the golf spectrum. Regardless of where you are in the process, this book can help you improve that casual Sunday round, that "Let's do business over a round of golf" experience, and make the competitive player sharper, confident, and more prepared.

- *Novice/beginner*: basically starting from scratch
- *Social Golfer*: enjoys being with friends, talking and getting caught up, and the beautiful scenery and fresh air

- *The Business Golfer*: realizes that many business opportunities can be made on the course; wants to walk the walk and talk the talk
- *Weekend Warrior*: no time during the week; hustles to the course on weekends to hit a few balls, a few putts and tee it up with his buddies
- *The League Golfer*: has some time to practice; plays a couple times a week; has had a few lessons from a local pro or buddy who is a good golfer; still has the burning desire to compete
- *The Serious Golfer*: practices a few hours a week; has a few golf books, DVD's and You Tube sites to learn about golf; has taken moderate instruction; plays in some tournaments; Can walk the walk and talk the talk; believes she/ he can always get better; would like to have more time to work at it
- *The Competitive Golfer*: devotes the time and energy to prepare for tournament golf; it is a part of who he is; has analyzed and taped his swing and compared his positions to others; has had considerable instruction; has goals and dreams to be a true tournament player

Where are you on the golf spectrum? Where do you want to be? How can we get you there?

"The toughest distance in golf is the six inches between the ears"

"Whether you think you can or think you can't, you're right!"- Henry Ford

"Ability is what you're capable of doing. Motivation determines what you do. Attitude determines how well you do it." - Lou Holtz

Section Reading Focus:

- What are my golf goals?
    - ○ _____
    - ○ _____
    - ○ _____

- How do I practice? What is my focus and routine?

- Do I have a pre- shot routine that puts me in the right mental state to hit the golf shot?

- Do I build myself up on the golf course and remain confident?

- Am I my own worst enemy on the golf course and commit self-sabotage?

- Am I comfortable with being a "low 80's" or "bogey golfer"? How do I break out of my comfort zone?

- Do you stay in the moment or do you let your mind wander to what has happened or what is going to happen? Stay "Present" focused.

With all the variety of golf swings that are out on various tours, obviously there is more than one way to get the ball in the hole. I have seen many golfers with less than perfect swings beat the heck out of golfers with beautiful, smooth, graceful swings. How? Why? They know how to get the ball in the hole! It is often said… it's not how, but how many! The belief in one's ability on the golf course; the self-confidence one possesses; the tenacity one holds within: those are the most powerful tools in golf. As Gio Valiente says, "It's fearless golf".

I have an ever-growing library of books and articles devoted to developing a stronger mental golf game. I've read every one of them and many of them three or four times. Of course, there is some redundancy but I've been fortunate to learn a great deal from these books and how to become stronger mentally. Part of my lesson structure is to talk to my students about their golf emotions and how they channel their focus and energy. No matter what level of player you are, you can improve your mental game. Whether I am teaching in my classroom or on the practice tee, I strive to get the most out of my students. I want to develop and reinforce their commitment, confidence, composure, and character.

The following pages and passages are a representation of the message that sports psychologists are sending not only to golfers but to many of today's sporting superstars as well. We can learn a lot from watching and listening to these people about overcoming odds and persevering through difficult competitive situations. The best thing is you don't have to be a superstar to apply them to your own game or sport.

A former high school player of mine, whom I still work with as a member of the PGA Canada Tour, and I were talking one day. He said that a lot of teams and players have talent but that very few coaches help each player realize his talent and build it into a reality. "Coach", this player said, "You can feel rest assured that you were able to get us to play to our potential and beyond more often than not. You made our talents into realities because of the way you coached us and motivated us." That, without a doubt, is the greatest coaching compliment I've ever received. I can't take all the credit on this. I was surrounded by teams of players who realized what commitment and dedication it took to get to the highest levels of success in high school golf. Many of these players went on to play at Division I, II and III colleges or enter professional golf/management programs. A few, like this player, have also challenged themselves to take it to the next level as a playing professional.

> *"You have to be one mentally tough dude to dominate at Golf."*
> *- John Gruden*

Quick Thoughts:

1. Golf is a game; it is meant to be enjoyed!
2. Fall in love with the process. Enjoy the process of getting better, putting in time, and overcoming obstacles. Golf takes

time and hours of practice. Part of the fun of golf has got to be the work, practice and effort to get better.

3. Harvey Penick says: "Take Dead Aim!" Be totally into your target.
4. What is my target? Be precise and specific.
5. Stay in the Present. You can't control what has happened and you don't know what is to come. Don't worry about what has happened and don't get ahead of yourself.
6. Tension kills a golf shot.
7. See, Feel, Trust: See the shot, feel the shot, trust your preparation and abilities- *"7 Days in Utopia"* (Great golf movie!)
8. See, Feel, Do- Nick Faldo
9. The Five P's: Practice + Patience + Persistence = Positive Performance
10. Make fearless swings at specific targets: Gio Valiente
11. Golf is played not by size, but by skill, intelligence, and guts.
12. Have positive body language. Walk with pride and conviction. Show your opponent and the course who is boss!

Which of these "quick thoughts" can you use today to put you in a positive mind set to go out and play great golf? Mental keys don't have to come from memorizing chapters in a book or articles in a magazine. Mental keys, like swing thoughts, need to snap you into playing gear and provide a positive direction to hit the right shot at the right time.

My Favorite quick thought is: _____

A quick thought that has worked for me in the past is:

_____

Other notes taken from this section:

GOAL SETTING

Players who have goals (a vision and dream of what they want and see themselves doing) generally outperform those without goals. In golf, goals make our practice and preparation purposeful, focused, and of a higher quality. Goals are targets that guide us to better preparation and a stronger performance. Goals need to be measureable, attainable, and changeable depending on circumstances.

At the start of every season you should make a list of goals that you want to accomplish in the short run that will benefit you and lead to your long range goals.

My (author) playing goals for 2015 are:

- Have fun playing and teaching golf
- Play more golf with my family
- Develop a relationship with a colleague that will support me mentally and physically in attaining my goals
- To be competitive and win on local Florida and State tours
- Win at least two events in my local association
- Qualify for the Florida State Open
- Finish my golf manual and get it published

My (author) playing goals for the future:

- Have fun playing and teaching golf
- Play more golf with my family
- Continue to be competitive in tournaments and my local association as I get older
- Play in some Senior State Events and hopefully some Champions Tour Events
- To become a "Complete Golfer" and know that I did my best to achieve that status
- Qualify for the U.S. Senior Open

Goals of Goal Setting:

- Make goals specific and reachable; they can be difficult but not unrealistic or impossible.
- Goals that a player sets for him/herself are more motivating than goals set for them by someone else.
  - Someone can help you set your goals (it is good to have a mentor/confidant). But, for the player to have success reaching those goals, he must own them.
- Goals need to be positive with a system or method laid out to reach them.
- Try to make goals process oriented.
  - "In order for me to win the club tournament, I will practice my short game 60% of my total practice time. I will use a specific short game practice check list to measure my results."
- Goals can be made and reached in increments or steps.
- Short term goals are better than long range goals. It is good to have both but you can't win the U.S. Open without attaining some other goals in the process.
- Accept constructive criticism/reinforcement/revision of your goals.
  - Meet with your mentor or confidant to go over your progress and discuss any problems or weaknesses you are having in achieving your goals.
- Think of a specific drill that can be implemented to get you past the roadblock preventing you from attaining that goal.
- Positively reinforce yourself as much as possible. Congratulate yourself when you attain a goal.
- Goals have to be written down, along with the plan on how to reach those goals.

Feel free to use this space to highlight and write down your goals. Try to come up with 2-3 short term goals and 2-3 long term goals. When you reach a goal, make a new goal. Golf is a process or journey that is always evolving. Never be satisfied. Always work to improve but also take the time to enjoy and celebrate a new milestone!

Example: My goal is to practice 15 hours per week. I will devote 6 hours to my long game on the range. I will devote 4.5 hours to my putting drills. I will devote 4.5 hours to wedges and greenside shots.

Short Term Goals:

1. _____
2. _____
3. _____

Long Term Goals:

1. _____
2. _____
3. _____

How did your goals work out? Success? If so, congratulations! If not, what can you do to bring about success the next time out?

PUTTING MENTAL PREPARATION INTO PRACTICE

One of the most difficult things for golfers is taking the mental and physical practice you do and applying it to the golf course. For me, I love to hit balls on the range. I love searching for the truth in my swing. However, I also realize that I need to spend more time playing golf and adjusting to all the choices that playing golf gives us (wind, club choice, shot shape, greenside shots, sloping putts, etc).

QUESTION: Do you feel that your time is spent more practicing or playing? Both are important but there has to be a balance.

Two Golf Modes

1) *Practice mode*: careful analysis of the routines and dynamics of the swing through drill and practice work
2) *Playing mode*: having the practice mode become so routine that you can make fearless swings at specific targets

Note: Work as hard as you can on the practice tee, short game area and green so you can free it up on the golf course.

It is impossible to take the practice mode to the golf course and expect to play well. Few golfers can think of more than 2 swing thoughts in a golf swing without causing physical and mental anxiety. This produces tension which negatively impacts the swing. Confidence can only be gained when the practice mode moves into the playing mode. This doesn't happen overnight. Remember this: When you are on the course you have to let yourself out of the practice mode of position and swing analysis and allow the body to flow in one smooth, athletic movement. As Jim Flick said "You have to play with vision, feel, and rhythm".

Individual Shot Analysis

Question: How much time do you spend on your pre-shot routine and post-shot analysis? How can you improve both of these?

In the last U.S. Open that Tiger Woods won, the analysts timed his putting pre-shot routine. He was within hundredths of a second of his usual routine over each putt every time. He took the same number of practice strokes; he had the same body language. He was totally into his routine which set up for some awesome putting.

Also, if you watch players on TV, you will see them hit a shot. If it is a great shot they may chase after it or pose until it lands. If it is a bad shot you will see them go through some post- swing simulations to get the right feeling in their body and mind before they hit the next shot. Since they don't get "mulligans" on tour, they try to envision or reenact what they want their perfect swing to be like on the next shot.

Here is a three step system to analyze your "on course play" and each individual shot. I've separated each shot into a series of three mini-events. *I think this is one of the most important sections of this entire manual.*

1. Pre-shot routine: Prior to the event: *Be Prepared*

- Have you done what it takes to perform at your highest level (practice, strategy, game plan)?
- Have you prepared physically and emotionally for the round?
- Have you set accurate, realistic, optimistic goals for your performance?
- Have your prepared your bag and self with the right gear and are you well fueled?
- Have you focused on 1 or 2 swing thoughts or sensations? Or do you have a checklist attached to your bag of 10 things you need to do to hit a golf ball? If you do throw it away! Learn how to simplify the process; it reduces tension!
- Have you established an effective pre-shot routine to prepare you for the athletic movement of hitting a golf ball and playing the game?
  - Repeat the same thing for each shot every time.
  - Focus on the target, visualize the swing and ball flight and take Dead Aim.
  - Breathe
- Commit to the shot and your decision.
  - Trust your calculations and judgment.
  - Trust your swing.
  - Stay in the present
  - Single minded focus

2. During the event: *Tension Free Swing*

- Target focus and allow your athletic ability to get the ball to your target
  - Do not see hazards: see where you want the ball to land and burn it into your brain.
  - Make your target the last thing you look at.
- Limited swing thoughts (develop positive swing sensations/ feelings)
- Relaxed, focused concentration

- No self-doubt
- The Swing
  - ○ Have faith in your own individual, unique swing- the one you are comfortable with and have developed (As Arnold Palmer says: "Play your own swing… I did").
  - ○ Keep swing thoughts to one or two at the most. The mind and body have to focus on the energy needed to produce an effortless swing that sends the ball to the target. Excess swing thoughts produce tension (this is something that I continually struggle with in my own game!).
    - □ **Instead of a swing thought, try to feel a swing sensation**: A swing sensation is a feeling of how you want the club to move or feel rather than forcibly putting it into positions.
    - □ I believe you can have numerous swing sensations, but few swing thoughts.
    - □ Your swing sensations should be felt in your waggle or preparatory move before you start the swing.
  - ○ Play; don't practice, during a scoring round.
  - ○ Trust what you have on that day and go with it. If the ball wants to fade a little, just go with it.
  - ○ **Present Focus:** The most important thing in life is what you are doing for the 3 seconds it takes to hit the shot. You can't think about what has already happened. You can't think about the future. Stay in the moment!

3. After the event- *Analyze*

- Learn from your shot.
- Swing rehearsal to get the right feel /sensation before the next shot
- Coach yourself to do it better next time.
- Maintain Composure and Confidence.
  - ○ Don't put too much emphasis on a good or bad shot.

- How you react to a shot - especially negative reaction - can influence your play for a long period of time. A strong negative reaction sits in our mind longer and hinders us from being positive on the next shot.
- Reward and cheer for yourself - to yourself - for a good shot. Positive vibes can carry us just as easily as negative vibes can destroy us.
- Scotch guard yourself; allow negativity to drip off you like raindrops off an umbrella.
- Accept the results and prepare and execute the next shot.
- Control what you can control (emotions, attitude, routine, strategy, preparation, practice).
- Don't worry about what you can't control (opponents, course condition, weather, luck).
- You can't do anything about a shot already played or a shot that hasn't been played. You are in control of the shot at hand. Don't look back and don't plan what you will do with the rest of the round (Stay in the moment)
- Adjust your mind set to be confident and fully prepared for the next shot
- Don't add to a mistake by making another one trying to make up for the one you just made.
- Remember your goals and keep working to achieve them.
  - It is good to set goals at the beginning of the round even though you may have to modify those goals during the round.

Describe your pre-shot routine:

Describe what you think over the ball:

Describe your post shot analysis:

POSITIVE SELF TALK AND MANTRAS

Question: Do you positively gear up for the shot? Do you get over the shot with a negative thought or fearful emotion? Do you see fairways and flagsticks or bunkers and hazards? What you last envision before you take the club back will most often guide the mind and body to complete it… good or bad!

PRE-SHOT AND SHOT "MANTRAS": Verbal golf and self-talk

In a recent tournament, I started 5 over par on the first 5 holes. I received a couple of really bad breaks that earned me a run of bogeys and a double. Not how I wanted to start off my tournament! At the end of the 5ᵗʰ hole, I had a little self-talk session. I said "Paul, you can have the woe-is-me attitude and resign to a poor round or you can bounce back, make a couple birdies and get back on track". At the end of the 16ᵗʰ hole I was back to two over par, feeling pretty good about myself; not the score as much as how I was able to condition my state of mind into a can-do rather than can't- do attitude. To finish the story… unfortunately some rain and thunder came in and I finished bogey – bogey. But this early in the season after a very long winter and terrible spring (lovely Wisconsin), I felt good that I could get my mental state of mind tournament ready and make mental adjustments during my round. It was just another step in the process of becoming a "Complete Golfer". **The Moral of the story? We are in control of how we think and act on the golf course!**

Another example: I took a quick November trip to Arizona to work with Neil Johnson who was preparing for the final stage of Q-School. I hadn't played for a month. We did a lot of range work but we also played 4 rounds of desert/mountain golf. I went down with the expectation of having fun and enjoying the time. I was in a good golf mind-set despite a long lay-off. I played the four rounds under par for the weekend. I only gave one ball to the desert. I didn't see the desert. I saw the middles of the fairways and the spot I wanted to land it on the greens. I was amazed at how simple it seemed. No tension, total control of what I was doing. I almost felt like a Complete Golfer!

Remind yourself that you can/will hit a good shot. Talk yourself into hitting a good shot.

1. Continually ask yourself: "What's my target"? Burn the image into your mind.
2. "See, feel, do" : See the shot (visualize); Feel the shot (practice swing or sensation); Execute the shot with total trust in your ability (Nick Faldo tip)
3. Develop your rhythm by repeating a cadence for good tempo (Sam Snead tip).
   - Waltz – backswing is 1,2 and impact is 3
   - Backswing is Er-nie and impact is Els
   - Backswing is A-dam and impact is Scott
   - Backswing is Jor-dan and impact is Speith
4. You may want to experiment using a metronome to get the cadence that works best for you and then practice with the metronome so the rhythm gets grooved in your brain. (There is an interesting book called *Tour Tempo* that describes this).
5. Say something confident and positive before your shot.
   - This is positive self-talk
   - Make a list of I will, I am, or I can statements to use to get you in the moment.
     - I am a great putter from 5 feet.
     - I am a great driver of the golf ball.
     - I will commit to this shot and focus on my target.
   - Play the shot in your mind. Talk yourself into hitting a good shot.
     - Verbal visualization- Like "Playing Lessons with the Pros" on the golf channel. Verbalize what you want to do. Enact the senses.
     - "I'm going to hit a 3 yard fade into that right pin location".
     - Talk yourself into hitting a great shot!

6. Develop a Mantra or "trust cue" (Winters) to get you ready for the shot.
    *   Mine is TRUST: target, routine, under stressful times
    *   R.K. Winters – FOCUS: focus, optimism, commitment, undivided attention, simplicity
7. Self Talk
    *   Be kind to yourself while on the golf course.
    *   You CAN talk yourself into a good shot or a bad shot.
    *   Don't beat yourself up. There are plenty of people who want to do that to you on the course.
    *   Don't let your beliefs limit your performance. Instead let them expand your performance to reach your potential. It's ok to dream!
        ○   Bob Rotella says there are no hot streaks. Hot streaks are just a glimpse into what our true potential is.
    *   Affirmations: a statement of fact or belief, positive or negative, that will lead to an end result.
        ○   Telling yourself that you will succeed and accomplish your goals is a good start to success. It is actually a vital component to success.
    *   *NOTE: your physical skills (practice, preparation) need to be developed, too. You can't just will something to happen.*
    *   Examples of affirmations:
        1. I am prepared; I am relaxed; I am focused on my target; I am a champion; I am fearless; I am a great putter; I know how to hit a pressure tee shot.
        2. Write out your affirmations and look at them often.
        3. Speak them out loud to incorporate more senses.
        4. Affirmations must be positive and to the point- a command.

Ask yourself: What can I do to incorporate positive self-talk into my pre-shot routine and during my round? How can I use what I've read to prevent myself from negative self-talk that leads to poor shots in the future?

Goal: Don't let a bad thought or shot effect the next one. Deal with it and move on!

REDUCING TENSION AND OVERCOMING FEAR

"I was so tight you couldn't a drove a flaxseed down my throat with a knot maul" - Sam Snead

Golf Fuel:

1. Good attitude = good fuel = good performance
2. Bad attitude= bad fuel = bad performance
3. YOU CAN CONTROL THE FUEL YOU PUT INTO YOUR BRAIN!

According to David Breslow in *Wired to Win,* there are four negative effects of tension in the swing:

1. Loss of power
2. Poor, shallow, quick breathing
3. Loss of feel in the short game
4. Tight muscles produce a tight, quick swing, putt, or chip

Tight muscles can't SWING a golf club. It is a golf swing, not a golf hit. The club needs to be swung, not directed. There needs to be fluidity, rhythm, and balance. The ultimate goal is to deliver the club to the ball in the right position at impact with maximum power while maintaining fluidity and rhythm.

- Self Check:
    - Do the veins in your arms pop out at address?
    - Are your knuckles white?
    - Do you squeeze the club instead of cradle it?
    - Is your mouth and jaw tight?
    - Are your legs stiff or locked?
    - Are your wrists stiff?
    - Do you try to control the club in the swing and force it into positions?

- **If you answered yes to any of these- you have a tension filled swing!**

What to do under a tense situation: Overcoming tension and fear in the Golf Swing

- Breath deep in through the nose out through the mouth (however, some will argue it should come out through your nose as well- main point is controlled, level breathing); let your jaw relax and shoulders and arms fall freely on the exhale. Allow your tongue to drop from the roof of your mouth. Under tension, the heart rate quickens. Deep breathing is the only way to slow down your heart rate so that you can get your emotions under control. It must be a part of any pre-shot routine.
    - Breathe in for a count of 5 and exhale for a count of 5 while visualizing the shot you want to play.
    - Find your "happy place" before you swing the club.
- Visualize- see the target, not the hazards. Hazards only exist in pre-shot analysis and then they must be blocked out. The more specific and real your visualization, the greater the chance for success.
- One of my best players never practiced out of a bunker. When I asked him why, his response was: "Why practice out of an area that I don't intend to be in?"
    - Now, this may be a bit flawed, but it shows complete commitment and confidence in his ability and visualization.
- Continually practice positive thoughts, affirmations, and self-talk.
- Stick with your routine. Make everything as mundane and emotionally flat as possible.
- Firm grip, soft arms. Feel the weight of the club head throughout your swing, almost like you were swinging a broom or weighted club.

- Focus on tempo, rhythm, balance- not swing thoughts and positions. Build some ideas of swing sensations that provide positive flow in the golf swing.
- When the mind is calm and focused, we can more easily focus on the desired results. That shot has to be the only thing on your mind for the 5 seconds surrounding impact.
    - Teach yourself to focus for 12 minutes!
        i. The average shot (pre shot, swing) takes about 10 seconds. If you shoot 80, that is 800 seconds. So the actual time you are actually engaged in "playing golf" is about 12 minutes.
        ii. The actual time to hit the shot it is about 3 seconds or 4-5 minutes per round. If you are able to compartmentalize for that period of time and totally commit for that period of time you will see better results.
    - Again; we are working on PRESENT focus. One shot and one thought at a time.
- Trust your ability and have faith in yourself.
- Remember it is golf- not life and death.
- **It is a game** to be played and enjoyed.

Questions:
- How is your body engaged for a shot?
- Are you stiff and tense?
- Are you fluid and relaxed?
- Do you go through breathing exercises?
- Are you focused on the target or the hazards?
- Do you trust your preparation, ability, and are you able to freely accept the outcomes and move on?
- Are you playing for yourself?
- Are you "Present" focused? Or is your mind racing. Calm body, calm mind; breathe

Thoughts: Describe how you feel over a shot and what you can do to calm your body and mind.

"I never really learned how to play golf until I learned how to breathe"-Tom Watson

This is a good place for some self- reflection. Close your eyes. Imagine yourself over a golf ball. Are you loose, fluid, and relaxed? Are you tense, nervous, and tight? Imagine backing away from the golf ball, taking a huge breath and exhaling. Now get back over the golf ball. Repeat as necessary to get into the moment.

The Four Letter Word: FEAR!!!

"Lets face it, 95% of this game is mental. A guy plays lousy golf, he doesn't need a pro; he needs a shrink!" – Tom Murphy

"Fear may be real but is no match for the committed, confident golfer" – Tiger Woods

Everyone has a hole or shot that causes tension or fear. Everyone has their "17 at TPC Sawgrass" or their first tee shot at the U.S. Open. For most of us it just might be a hole that we are not comfortable with or the first tee shot when everyone is watching. It is okay to feel nerves and excitement but our goal here is to not approach that shot or hole with fear.

Discover first what you are fearful of:

1. Fear of embarrassment?
2. Fear of performing poorly?
3. Fear of losing?
4. Fear of not meeting your expectations or goals?
5. Fear of losing your swing?
6. Fear of not being respected?
7. Fear of playing bad in front of parents or spectators?

To help conquer those fears or other fears you have to put it in perspective: Remember, you must play for yourself and to reach your goals. You can't play for other people or the expectations they have for you. Appreciate the fact that you have people interested in you and what you are trying to accomplish.

- In my years of coaching and teaching golf, I have seen this all too often from parent to player. Again the parent's job is to support and encourage!
- THE PLAYER PLAYS, THE COACH COACHES, AND THE PARENTS SUPPORT

8. *For high school coaches and parents: I think it is important for the coach to step in and meet with the parents and describe the type of influences they can have on a kid in a round of golf (that goes for coaches, too, so be wary of what you say and do). This can be seen and heard by the player in both verbal and non-verbal communication and the "over-analysis" that takes place after a round in which the kid played poorly. Kids have to play for themselves first and they have to enjoy what they are doing. I never let my players apologize to me or anybody else for a round of golf unless it was for something not related to the physical playing of the game (poor sportsmanship, unsupportive of teammates, losing composure, cheating….). I also tried to get rid of negative thoughts immediately whether it was before, during, or after a round.*

    - *Example: I had a team at the state tournament a number of years ago. We were the best team in the state and on the first day of the tournament we shot a team score of 289; 1 over par. We ended the day with a 13 shot lead over the next closest team. No team had ever shot under 295 in the state tournament before. We felt good about our position; the parents and team were on cloud nine. Two things happened:*

        i.   *First: One of my players was quoted in the local newspaper that "We had this in the bag, no team would touch us". I'm all for confidence but it must be inward confidence. What happened in effect is a challenge was thrown out to the other teams; a nothing to lose day coming up for them. It also added pressure on us to hold up our end of the deal. Adding this pressure created some tension. People made comments about the quote. It fueled some other teams' fires.*

        ii. *Second: As the second day progressed, we weren't playing as well and as we made the turn on the back 9 some teams had gained on us. My team was tight. The parents were nervous. I was trying to do damage control on the course but that is no easy job. I could only talk to the players from green to tee. I was probably a little shell shocked as well.*

What I saw was that as my team hit a poor shot or missed a putt, their heads were going down, their posture was changing; they were getting defensive- not trusting their ability. The parents responded in kind with head shaking, moans and groans, disbelief, anxiety (none of them did anything mean, unsportsmanlike, or cruel) and just negative energy all around us. Negative energy is bad golf fuel. It spreads like a sickness on the team. On the reverse side, the other teams were feeling the excitement and positive energy of getting back in the tournament. Their fans and parents were cheering and fist pumping. That further led to the frustration of my team and parents.

iii. *In the end, we lost by one shot. We didn't play terrible. We shot 306. We set a new tournament record, but it just so happens, so did one other team!*

iv. *I think there came a point in that second round where we became afraid. We became more afraid of losing, than confident in winning. We thought more about what people would say if "We blew a 13 shot lead" than sticking to our game plan and riding out the storm. I don't put that on the players at all. That was my job as coach; to help them weather the storm. I may have been able to do more if we had today's coach/player rules in effect then.*

v. *The lesson here is that we need to remain supportive and positive on the course. Golf is a game of ups and downs and swings in momentum. It is imperative that you have a system in place that gets you out of the lows quicker and back to your normal game. We are not always in control of good days and bad, and we are certainly not in control of luck. We have to be prepared to face the challenges that golf gives us and not give up. My players didn't give up. We/I just didn't have a good enough system in place to deal with the challenges of handling the press, course, and emotional requirements that faced us at that time.*

Thoughts on Fear:

- Fear and anxiety cause tension which leads to many negatives in golf.
- Tension and stress come from fear; tension and stress don't allow you to swing the club freely.
- It is ok to be nervous, not ok to be fearful.
- "Fear limits us, confuses us, and causes us to achieve less than our abilities otherwise would allow"- Gio Valiente.
- Also, according to Valiente, there are four ways that fear affects us:
  - Fear produces tension which produces a tight grip which leads to tight muscles.
  - Fear makes us too quick from the top of the swing.
  - Fear causes deceleration and steering.
  - Fear causes us to come out of the shot.
- Overcoming fear? Re-read the earlier section on overcoming tension.
  - Make fearless swings at specific targets.
  - Confidence! Confidence! Confidence!
  - Stay in the moment. Here is an excerpt of Adam Scott's remarks after winning the 2013 Masters.
    - "The thing I did well today was stay right where I was. I didn't think about what happened in the past". That is great present focus.
  - Focus on the process, not the outcome.
  - Execute to the best of your ability; play the percentages and keep the odds in your favor; play the shot you are comfortable with given the circumstances.
  - Trust your preparation and your ability.
  - Be proud of who you are whether you hit a good shot or a bad shot.
  - Golf is a game of misses. We miss more shots than we perfect. If you can accept that you will be able to move on at a quicker and more meaningful pace.

> – It's not how good your good shots are it's how good your bad shots are. Narrow your miss region and you will see quicker improvement in your scores.

Discover what you are afraid of. Devise a plan (goals) to overcome that fear. It won't happen overnight but fear can be reduced with positive self-talk, affirmations and self-confidence.

Exercise: List below what you can do next time you play to reduce fear and tension in your golf swing. It might be as simple as correct breathing, visualization, or positive self talk.

COMFORT ZONES: Do you have a picture of the player you want to be?

Question: How do you refer to yourself as a golfer? Are you a "mid-80's shooter"? Are you a "bogey" golfer? Giving yourself a "title" of the golfer you are keeps you stuck in that rut. If you are a "bogey" golfer, you need to start thinking of yourself as a "mid-80's shooter". You will need to do some full game analysis to find your weakest areas; work on them; and then make them stronger in order to get rid of the old title and aspire and work towards a new one. In other words, How do you change your mind set to go from a "Mid-80's" player to a "High 70-s" player?

A comfort zone is a scoring range in which a golfer is comfortable shooting. They don't get too nervous or anxious at the low end of the comfort zone; they don't get too angry or frustrated at the upper end of the zone. You'll often hear a golfer say "I'm a mid 80's shooter." When that golfer has a chance to shoot in the mid 70's is when the problems start - nerves, stress, and anxiety. That golfer is out of his/her comfort zone and strange things can happen.

Comfort zones make it nearly impossible to shoot a low score. Golfers must break free of their comfort zone. Comfort zones become a problem when a golfer plays better than expected or is breaking new ground. You may have started out like you were going to shoot your personal record, thinking that you finally figured it out. Mentally, you realize that you have this great opportunity and that you are in uncharted territory. Ideally, what you want to do is keep riding it. Realistically, what we normally do is self-sabotage it. We can't get out of our own way (Take a look at Adam Scott in last years British Open vs. this year's Masters). You started off with a string of pars and then got to the 6th hole and went double, bogey, double- back into your comfort zone. The key is to never think about the final score. Just keep doing what you are doing and focus on the process, not the end result. When you get the chance to "go-low", GO LOWER!!!!

Example: For a number of years, you could mark me down for a score of 70 to 74. I was frustrated that I had never broken 70. I knew that I could and should do it. I had been 3 or 4 under par many times but then limped in with some bogies to shoot 70 or 71…. Or even worse! When I finally did break 70 it was with a 66. My next three rounds were 68, 69, 69. Once you break the barrier, you will retrain your mind to do things you haven't been able to do before. It becomes easier and your belief in your ability grows. You have new standards and goals. Remember: low scores aren't a hot streak… they are only a glimpse of what we are truly capable of accomplishing (Bob Rotella).

Break Out of Your Comfort Zone: Think of yourself as the player you want to be!

- Prepare: Know the course, plan your strategy based on your strengths and abilities, practice for success.
- Positive self-talk: Talk yourself into playing well; one bogey won't destroy a round.
- Target oriented: Repeat your thoughts about strategy and target and swing to it.
- Visualize
    o See, feel, Do!
    o Repeat your mantras to stay in the right frame of mind.
    o See where you want the ball to go- not where you don't want it to go.
- **Stay in the present**: Focus all of your attention and energy on the shot you are playing, not about a previous bad shot or the next shot. Commit to the shot you are hitting and to the target
    o *"You just have to stay in the moment. Golf is one shot at a time. You cannot live in the past. You have to play the shot at hand. That's what I've always done" - Tiger Woods*
- Deal with the distractions, whether they are your playing partners, weather elements or hazards, in a positive way. CONTROL WHAT YOU CAN CONTROL!
- Stick with your routine and mannerisms.
- Break the limitations you put on yourself. THINK BIG!
- Train your brain to perform at its peak level. You can hit all the practice balls in the world, but if your brain isn't ready you won't perform at your peak level.
- Muscles can't actually remember but your brain can! Work on swing sensations and feelings that you can copy and replicate.
- Relax and Breathe. Get your internal motor under control.
- Have self-trust and appreciation; not self-doubt and degradation.
- Be Committed, Confident, Composed.
- Improve your misses- The person with the best misses, wins!
- DEVELOP A GREAT SHORT GAME: Remember it's not how, but how many!

In order to break out of my comfort zone I am going to do these three (or more) things:

1. _____
2. _____
3. _____

For me, and the students I have who are stuck in that zone, I get them try a few different things:

- Play the forward tees to make more birdies.
- Play a few easier golf courses to regain confidence.
  - I like to hear when golfers go play easier courses and say that it helps them get "healthy"; it helps them regain confidence.
- Play their course more aggressively a few times; change up their game plan.
  - This also makes it fun and provides risk/reward situations.
- Make their weakest areas their strongest
- Reduce shots from 100 yards and in (Be a killer in the "Scoring" Zone)
- **MOST IMPORTANT**- you have to envision and strive to be the player you want to be.

HOW TO SCORE LOWER

Question:
- What is your lowest score ever?
- How did you shoot that score that day? What skills did you possess that were stronger than normal?
  - Remember, those skills are always there; we just have to unleash them more often.
- What was your mental attitude that day?
- What gets in the way from you shooting low scores more often?
  - Is it mental or physical

"To be a champion, you have to find a way to get the ball in the cup on the last day". - Tom Watson

Scoring lower? I assume that is a goal we all want to achieve. In bowling, perfection is 300. In golf, perfection is 18. I would say that score is unattainable, especially since the lowest recorded tour round is 59 on any of the major tours. Will someone go lower? Annika Sorenstam and her coaches believe in "Vision 54" - the concept that someone will actually make the equivalent of 18 birdies- a score of 54. Ben Hogan did dream one night that he did shoot that perfect score of 18. Nonetheless, the goal of every golfer is to Go Low!

There are four things to focus on to break 80 (and I think to play better overall):

1. Practice your short game (THE SCORING ZONE)
    - Over half of our shots are with wedges, chipping and putting.
    - Two-thirds of your practice time should be spent on shots under 100 yards.
      o This is what I refer to as the scoring zone: Maximizing your potential with your wedges and putter.
    - For details how to do this see the practice sheets and forms in the appendix.
2. Play the Necessary Shot, not the miraculous/heroic shot.
    - Odds are not in your favor to pull it off and the result could be a huge number.
    - Keep your ego in check.
    - Don't compound a bad shot with another bad shot.
    - If you're going to lay-up, then make sure you lay-up!
    - The dumbest question is asking a playing partner what club they hit (and it's a rules infraction). Play your own game to your own strengths.
    - There are such things as good bogeys. You can make up for a bogey or two but not for a double or two.
    - 7/10 rule: Hit the shot you would be safe with 7 out of 10 times.

- However: Don't be afraid during one of your casual rounds to hit driver every hole; play more aggressive to par 5's and short, tight par 4's and challenge yourself to make more birdies.

3. Focus on the process, not the outcome.
    - Play the course in chunks- it's easier to maintain present focus.
        o Chunks of three holes
        o Puzzle: Each shot is a piece of the puzzle. Don't lose any pieces and the puzzle will look good at the end.
        o Point A to Point B - one shot at a time
    - See the positive targets, not the negative targets.
    - Focus on what you have control over:
        o Your emotions, decisions, attitude, and self-talk
        o Your rhythm and your breathing
        o Your tempo and your timing
        o Your routine

4. Maintain a quality practice regimen with all of your clubs.
    - Adequate drill and practice work on the range
    - Developing positive swing sensations or feelings rather than swing thoughts.
    - Hitting multiple shots from a variety of lies and distances on the course

5. Other factors to consider:
    - Improve your strength, flexibility, and conditioning.
    - Improve mental conditioning (see list of good mental golf books in appendix).
    - Set goals instead of expectations.

Question: What is your par?

I've often thought about this. For a tour professional, their par may be 68 or 69 depending on the course and event. For me, my par is 71. For my Dad, his par is 86 (that matches his age and he has broken par more times than me in the past few years!) The point here is that most golfers can't go out and shoot the course par. We need to find a score we are comfortable with, achieve that score consistently, and then reduce par (reset goals). To reduce your par, you need to work on the weaknesses and inconsistencies that keep you from improving.

Note: Ultimately, we are who we believe we are and we do what we believe we can do. If you have aspirations and goals, and you work hard to achieve them, you will.

PHYSICAL GOLF

PREPARE YOUR BODY FOR BETTER GOLF

THE COMPLETE GOLFER:

PHASE TWO: DEVELOPING YOUR PHYSICAL GAME
Get Loose, Get Strong, Play Better!

In this section, you will learn about the following areas:
- How various body parts and dynamics impact the golf swing
- What body parts need to be flexible and strong to enhance golf swing dynamics
- Winter swing conditioning
- What you can do to improve your "golf body"

Section Reading Focus:

- Do you have the right equipment for your best golf?
- Do you understand how the body works in your golf swing?
- Do you spend time working on your flexibility?
- Do you spend time working on the body parts that will allow you to swing correctly, with more speed, control, and power?
- Is your body cardio-fit enough to reduce fatigue during a round of golf?
- Do you use the proper nutrition and hydration during a round of golf?

Self-Check: Where are you? Where do you want to get to?

- I can touch my toes with straight legs.
- Sitting on the floor, bottoms of feet facing each other and touching, I can push my knees to the ground.
- Sitting on the floor with my legs straight out, I can rotate my torso 45 degrees both ways.
- I can clasp my hands behind my back and push my arms behind me.
- Lying down on my back, I can press my hips into the air.
- I can do push-ups, crunches, lunges, squat holds/wall sits, one-legged balances.
- I can turn my upper body over a resisted lower body while keeping my head steady.

If these maneuvers are difficult for you then you will have trouble getting the club and body to consistently move in the right dynamics for maximum power and control. The rest of this section will give you some advice on how you can create a better body for golf.

I suggest you take some mental or physical measurements of how well or how far you can move and record them. With some time and effort you will see more flexibility and improvement in your golf game.

What's the best Method?

The debate is still out as to where the greatest gains in golf have been made over the last thirty years. Some say it is in technology; some say mental conditioning; some say physical conditioning; and others say it is instruction. Whatever it is, there is no question that the game of golf has made huge strides in popularity and playability. To play your greatest golf you have to examine all the above areas and explore how they apply to your game. It is impossible to reach peak performance in golf without being in good physical and mental condition. It is impossible to reach peak performance in golf without having the right set of clubs. It is impossible to reach peak performance in golf without having the proper instruction.

Here are four questions I want you to ask yourself in total assessment of your game:

1. Do I have the best set of clubs for my swing at a price that I am comfortable with?
2. Do I have the best instruction that I can get at a price that I am comfortable with?
3. Am I in the best physical shape that I can be in in order to achieve the proper swing mechanics and the mental and physical expectations of golf?
4. Do I have the right mental attitude and awareness to approach every shot with a positive frame of mind?

If you answered no to any of these, you know you have something more to consider as you try to become a "Complete Golfer".
This section will discuss what I feel to be the key ingredients in getting your body set up to play better golf. This includes flexibility, strength, and stamina or cardio-conditioning. Please keep in mind that I'm not a personal trainer. If you have the time and money I would recommend having one. Most of what I do and say is based on my own research through practice and development of my swing and the swings of hundreds of my students. It is what I've learned through analysis of

DVD, books, TV, and internet. I've developed and redeveloped my own program based on my own research.

There are also many classes available at gyms and training studios that teach Yoga, Tabata, Zumba, Cross-fit and many other programs as well. Find a trainer who can build a program to get your body into "Complete Golfer" golf shape! While you work to get stronger, you must also maintain or improve your flexibility.

Focus on these body areas for increased strength and flexibility:

Hamstrings, Quads, Core:

- Helps hold posture and support body. Someone with tight hamstrings will not be able to hold posture through the swing; especially at impact.
- Helps with load and turn and rotation through swing.
- Helps improve the differential between upper body turn and stable lower body (Jim McLean refers to this as the X-factor).
- Tremendous power source.

Hip Joints, Flexors, IT band:

- Allows us to pivot, load and rotate in our golf swing.
- Allows us to set up in correct posture and retain that posture in swing.

Chest and Back:

- Allows us to create turn and support the position of the upper body and arms.
- Allows us to properly set up in correct posture.
- Great power source.
- Ankles, Feet, Knees:
- Allows us to support the swing and remain grounded.
- Allows us to support the speed and torque that is created in the swing.
- Promote a good finish position through proper footwork.

Forearms, wrists, hands

- Allows us to hinge, unhinge correctly in the swing.
- Allows proper face rotation/motion of club head.
- Allows us to supply speed and power at impact.
- Allows us to feel the movement of the club during the swing.

Cardio Conditioning:

Strength and flexibility improvement is crucial to good golf. However, you need to adopt a cardio routine that will build endurance and stamina for the long hours and walks on the golf course. Good physical conditioning is also related to stronger mental conditioning. If the body isn't as tired, the mind won't be as tired. And, most importantly, it will improve your overall quality of life!

When you think of the golf swing, there are hundreds of movements that have to be timed perfectly in order to hit a decent golf shot (Bob Rotella refers to an accurate golf shot as a minor miracle!). Being in good physical shape and being flexible and strong will help all these moving parts connect at the right place and time or, at least, will increase the odds of it all happening at the right place and right time.

WORKOUT IDEAS

Flexibility: You need to have a well rounded stretching routine based on _proper practice_. I can't tell you how many times someone has come to a lesson and "stretched". Watching them go through their routine, I only hoped they didn't hurt themselves before the lesson began!

I recommend starting every day off with a 15 + minute stretching routine/warm-up. You should also develop some good pre-round stretches that focus on breathing, stretching, and calming the mind. I HIGHLY recommend a good yoga practice 2-4 times per week. Swinging with a medicine ball or weighted club will help loosen and strengthen the golf muscles (You can also look at a speed stick, swingrite trainer, Orange Whip, swing fan or other online options).

Stretching focus: breathing; relaxed mind and body; smooth transitions and stretches

- Hamstrings and calf muscles
- Side stretches
- Hips and quads
- Chest opener
- Low back, neck, upper back
- Shoulders, forearms, wrists
- Rotational: Upper body turn against a stable lower body; the shoulders turn about 45 degrees and the hips half of that or hold the hips completely and do torso turns

Strengthening focus:

- Legs: quads, hamstrings, calves (load, coil, stability)
- Core: glutes, abdominals, lower back, obliques (load, posture, coil)
- Back: upper and lower back (posture, turn, rotation)
- Arms, wrists, forearms, shoulders (club control, hinge)
- Ankles, feet (balance and stability)
- Winter Swing Conditioning: These can be used anytime to maintain strength and flexibility in the season as well.
- Work on flexibility and strengthening as needed
- Building swing sensations or simulations
  - Swing an evenly weighted club (momentus, power hitter, swingrite, Orange Whip). Swing 10 times from the left side and 10 times from the right (it is important to do your exercises bi-laterally). Build up to 20-30 reps from each side- building speed with increasing reps. Make sure the swing is the loudest through the impact area

○ I recommend getting a swing fan and completing the same action as in #1 above. The swing fan is a great swing aid as it allows you to make a swing simulation while building speed and increasing your cardio rate. You can build hand, forearm, and wrist strength by making short, quick swings (like hitting the inside of a tire or garbage can)

a. Shadow swings: Make slow motion full golf swings to develop the proper swing movements or sensations that you want in your golf swing. You can record these or use a full length mirror to watch yourself making these swings.
b. Make swings using a medicine ball: Use your core muscles to control the movements. Play catch from a golf stance and swing position with a partner focusing on posture, coil, core, release.
c. Make swings off balance disks or half foam roller (swimming noodle). This is great for balance and stability and initiates your core.

Physical Golf Goals:

I will improve flexibility by doing the following:

1. _____
2. _____
3. _____

I will improve my physical strength by doing the following:

1. _____
2. _____
3. _____

I will improve my cardio-conditioning by doing the following:

1. _____

2. _____

3. _____

Suggestion/Reminder- Consult a professional trainer for one or more sessions to build a strength and flexibility routine to avoid injury.

Additional notes/thoughts from this section:

MECHANICAL AND INSTRUCTIONAL TECHNIQUES

THE COMPLETE GOLFER

PHASE 3: MECHANICAL AND INSTRUCTIONAL TECHNIQUES
Swinging the club with consistency, trust, and confidence!

In this section you will learn about the following areas:
- Core components of the golf swing
- Common Swing errors and the type of shot they produce
- Fundamentals of GASP
- Discussion of desired positions in the swing
- Note: I'm referring to right handed golfers in this section

Section Reading Focus:

- Do you have the proper fundamentals of grip, alignment, stance and posture?
- Are you in the right positions at set up, top of swing, impact, and finish?
- Do you have a swing flaw that produces undesired results?

- How do I get into good swing positions without losing the rhythm and feel of my swing?

FULL SWING

Please remember: This manual is a compilation of all I've read, watched, learned and figured out in my golf life. I don't hold the market on golf instruction. I created this manual to simplify your journey to becoming a "Complete Golfer". I highly recommend that you search out a qualified instructor and investigate on your own behalf what methods and strategies work for you.

The game of golf is a combination of physical, mental, and emotional components. To play your best golf and become a "Complete Golfer" you have to develop all areas. All three areas need to be in tune for a good shot, a good hole, a good round, and consistency over a long period of time. Pre-shot routines and thoughts or sensations, the swing (rhythm, timing, positions), and post shot analysis and behavior all contribute to your success. Seemingly good swings can and will produce poor shots if the mental aspect is not prepared and ready. So, as you go on the journey of becoming a "Complete Golfer", I want you to realize that there is more to curing a slice than "rolling the wrists at impact".

Core components to my teaching philosophy:

1. Fundamentals (GASP)
   - Grip, Alignment, Stance, Posture

2. Triangles
   - Formation formed by the arms and shoulders at address to produce the proper width and connection of the swing.
   - Proper leg position at address

3. Connection
   - Maintaining the connection of the arms and body throughout the swing

4. Load/Turn
   - Correct weight shift, pivot, coil, and torso rotation in the backswing

5. Rotational speed
   - Uncoiling the body's stored energy through the swing (from backswing pivot through to finishing pivot)

6. Impact
   - Proper position to deliver the club to the ball

7. Finish
   - The result of a well-sequenced golf swing

8. Rhythm, Balance, Feel

The flow, timing, and grace of our perfect swing

Common Swing Errors

In the golf swing, there are hundreds of moving body parts trying to find the right spot at "The moment of Truth".

"Hitting a good golf shot is a minor miracle!"- Bob Rotella

Some common swing errors:

1. Hitting from the top/over the top produces pulls, slices, and fat shots
2. Reverse pivot or tilt indicates improper weight transfer or shift (improper load in backswing).
3. Lack of shoulder turn and width in swing reduces power.
4. Disconnection of arms from body produces excess lift and poor contact and direction.
5. Falling back at impact produces fat, thin, and weak shots.
6. Losing posture causes thin shots.
7. Flat or Upright swing plane can lead to numerous issues.

It is nearly impossible to address all the areas that could cause the above problems. Below you will find some techniques and aids I use to fix faulty swing mechanics. Although, this manual is a "Self-Help" resource, I certainly recommend and have discussed the importance of having a support team. These may include a trainer, a caddy, a swing instructor, and of course a supporting family. Becoming a "Complete Golfer" is not a sprint. It is a marathon that will require long hours of practice, assessment, training, and competing. The biggest question to ask your self is: "Can I do this?" Can you commit to the process? If not, then I'm not saying give up. Find an area that you can develop with the time that you have to put into it. Adjust your goals based on your desired outcome. Can we all become "Complete Golfers"? I don't have the answer to that. But I do know that we can all improve given our time, resources, and commitment.

Question:

-   In your golf swing, what would you most like to fix (A position? A feeling?)
    -   What do you know to be wrong, and struggle to fix?
-   Do you generally hit a fade or slice? Draw or hook? Straight?
    -   Are you happy with your ball flight regarding trajectory and shape?
-   Do you struggle with balance and finish?
-   Do you have a "hitch" in your swing that other's comment on?

- Do you have a good swing but don't get the desired contact or results?
- Which way do your divots points and how deep or shallow are they?

Ultimately, you have to believe that you have the best swing on the planet. A swing that repeats itself under pressure and one you know you can draw from time after time.

- Jim Furyk was once asked the question: "How do you feel about that loop in your swing?" Furyk responded to this effect: "What loop? I have one of the best swings on the tour"! And the amount of money he makes would prove that!! Most importantly, he believes in himself, his swing, and his talent!

Focus on the fundamentals: GASP- grip, alignment, stance, posture

To me, a majority of the errors in a swing result from a problem in GASP!

These are tough to explain and I suggest you use one of the instructional resources found in the appendix for a visual presentation on GASP. Of course, I always recommend you find a teaching professional to work with as well.

The Grip (right handed golfer):

1. On a scale of 1-10, with 10 being a death lock on the club and 1 being the club falling out of your hands, the top hand (control hand) should be a 6 or 7 with the most pressure in the last 3 fingers. This would be firm, but not tight. The bottom hand (release hand) should be about a 4 or 5.
2. The club should be held more in the fingers with 2 or 3 knuckles visible on the control hand and the thumb just on

the other side of the grip (1:00 for a right hander). The fingers should also control the grip on the release hand and the right thumb pad should cover the control hand thumb. Never grip the club in the palms of your hand.

3. The V's of each hand (made by thumb and forefinger) should point to or slightly right of the chin for a right handed golfer. They need to be directly opposite of each other. The pressure should rest in the middle two fingers of the release hand. DO NOT PINCH the club with the thumb and forefinger. The golf grip is a fingers grip…. Not a palms grip!

4. There should be no tension in the hands and arms. You should be able to easily move the club with your wrists up and down and left and right.

5. The player should be able to make a loud swoosh at the bottom of a tension-free swing.

6. Try to maintain the same grip pressure in the swing. However it is natural for the hands to firm up at impact.

7. You can practice your grip with a specially designed grip that has grooves to put your fingers on or a yard stick to get your hands matching at address position.
    - I also recommend getting a weighted club with a specially designed grip to place your hands on the club correctly (Momentus).
    - A swing fan with the proper training grip is also an excellent practice aid.

Alignment/Aim:

1. Many mistakes can be made in a swing just as a result of poor alignment.

2. Main key: parallel alignment
    - Club face points to target or intermediate target (a spot about 3 feet in front of the ball is easier to line up to then a flagstick 150 yards away from you).
    - Feet are perpendicular to a square club face's bottom edge

- o Shoulders, hips, knees, eyes are parallel to feet.
- o Trail foot is perpendicular (could be a few degrees turned out) to the target line and the front foot is pointed out about 20 degrees.
- You may find that you are a little more closed on longer clubs to promote a sweeping motion and a little more open on short irons for a descending action at impact.
- You should always place alignment aids on the ground when you are practicing to reinforce proper aim.

Stance and Posture

1. Ball position: I never want any ball back of center on normal swings. I prefer that the wedges start from center of stance to just in front of belt buckle up to a driver being teed off your left arm pit. If the ball position is too far back in your stance it can lead to a poor load, tilt, or sway in the backswing and being too steep at impact or, conversely, a swing that is too in-to-out.
2. Posture: Also known as "Structure"
    - Angular in dimension
        - o Back straight
        - o Butt out/bend at hips
        - o Chin up
        - o Arms extended/hanging from shoulders
        - o Knees slightly bent
        - o Athletic/relaxed
    - Arms hang from shoulders in a relaxed manner, but more on top of the chest (I like to teach the triceps connected to the pectorals or no air/space in the tops of the arm pits). This gives a feeling of having the arms connected to the body.
        - o Right elbow is relaxed, a little bent.
        - o Try hitting shots with a glove under your left arm (right handed golfer) to get the proper connection in the backswing. The glove

shouldn't fall out until after impact. You can also try hitting shots with tees in each armpit.

a. On an iron shot, the end of the grip is about a fist length from the zipper and for a driver it is about a fist and an open thumb length from the zipper.

b. Weight is balanced on the arches of the feet and the feet are rooted to the ground. Never put weight on the outside edges of the feet or toes.
   ○ I believe that weight should be shifted somewhat left on all shots but more for short irons and progressively less for longer clubs.
   ○ I also recommend turning your head behind the ball at address (or feel like your nose is behind it).

c. Shoulders should be fairly level, but the release hand side might be a little lower.

If you have the proper GASP, improvement will be more rapid. If you struggle with these basic fundamentals, the body will try to develop counter-measures (bad habits) to fix the set-up problems.

Question: What should I look for in a Golf Professional?

Again, I always recommend going to your local teaching or club professional for lessons. However, do some checking on their philosophy, theory, price, experience, and method before you sign up. Furthermore, be wary of the playing partner that wants to offer you "advice". While there are many experienced players out there who may have sound advice, the average weekend golfer will not be of much useful assistance to you. Rarely is there a "quick-fix" to a problem. There may be "band-aids" that will help in the short run but those are not usually permanent fixes.

Golf coaches: If you are not an experienced professional or swing mechanic, please be careful when helping your players. Encourage them to get lessons or set aside some of your budget money to have a swing teacher come in for a clinic and work with your players. One of the most important things a parent or high school golf coach can do is set up focused practice sessions including attention to basic fundamentals, chipping, pitching, putting, and driving range. Remember that 60% of the practice time should be devoted to 100 yards and closer to the pin. I call this the "The Scoring Zone". PRACTICE WITH PURPOSE!

Triangles and Connection

1. At address, the arms chest and shoulders should form a triangle. You want to maintain that triangle feel at the beginning of your takeaway, allowing the chest and arms to move the club back first, followed by the hips and lower body. The backswing starts from the top down (shoulders, chest, arms) while the downswing starts from the bottom up (feet, knees, hips).

2. Connection occurs when the triceps stay connected to the pectorals (no air in upper armpits) throughout the swing until the finish. The feeling is like having a belt tied around your shoulders or a metal rod through your shoulders and armpits. This allows you to rotate around your spine. This feeling reduces excessive lift of the arms which can produce numerous swing flaws.

    • Note: there is some lift of the arms but if you keep a steady head, turn your chest away, stay connected, hinge your wrists correctly, and keep the club in front of your chest you will be in a great backswing position

    • You can feel connection with a glove under the arm pit of the lead arm or try a tee in each arm pit. You shouldn't lose the glove or tees until after impact

    • I've hit thousands of golf balls with a soft belt tied around my shoulders. Using the belt is effective from chipping to driving.

- AND... I don't care what I look like on the range with a belt tied around my shoulders. If someone pokes fun at me, I just need to say "O.K. come and beat me!

Load/Turn/Coil

1. Occurs with the correct weight shift or "Pivot" into the braced back leg. Weight shifts into the back heel, thigh, hip, and gluteal cheek. Front shoulder has turned to or behind the ball. Head has remained relatively steady (It is ok for head to shift laterally back- but not up, down, or forward)
   - Feel like you are starting the swing with your chest and arms together with the left arm staying close to the chest.
2. A feeling of stored power and energy ready to explode into ball
   - Because your weight has been set up slightly left you will be able to create torque, or differential between the upper and lower body which creates speed and power
   - Even though you have stayed left, or "stacked", you are still loading and coiling. You should feel pressure in the right side of your body; especially the right hip, butt cheek, and right heel.
   - Completely staying left, or tilting left will cause major swing issues
3. The right knee can work back a little but should not rotate out. The left knee, depending on core flexibility will remain stable (that keeps you stacked on the ball which will improve impact position) The left knee for a right handed golfer can also move back towards the ball to increase turn and pivot. Be careful of lifting the left heel off the ground too much.
4. *At the top of your backswing, your hands should be in front of your chest with arms extended (width), and your sternum should be turned away from the target; your head is on or just slightly behind the ball; and your elbows are pointed down; your hips are*

turned about one-third to one-half as much as your shoulders/ chest. You should still remain in good golf posture!

Impact

1. Defined by Jim Mclean as "The Moment of Truth".
2. You have seen many great players with different swings, but if you look at all of them at impact you will see some constants.
   a. Staying in your structure/posture at impact
   b. Weight shift to the front side with hips opening to target
   c. Your body is turning through the ball, not sliding into the ball
   d. Moving into and through the ball without stopping at impact
      ○ I often tell my students it is a golf swing not a golf hit. You need to allow your body to release and swing with maximum fluidity through the ball
   e. Shaft of club leading the club head (shaft lean) producing a descending strike and divot
   f. Back of top hand on grip facing the target with a square clubface
      ○ I prefer to teach the release of the hands through the ball with a left (leading) forearm rotation rather than throwing (casting) the trail hand to the ball at impact.
3. Your head has remained stable and is over or slightly behind the ball

Finish

1. Extension and release of body to target
2. Weight over your "hole-side" foot and rear heel straight up in the air
3. Belt buckle facing target

4. Arms folding over front / lead shoulder
5. Club shaft finishes across neck or shoulders
6. Maintain spine angle through impact and into finish (slight lean right in finish position)

Balance, Rhythm, Feel

1. The ability to maintain and hold the finish position
2. The swinging of the club with fluidity and liquidity
   - If you lose your balance in your swing/finish you are swinging too hard or have some bad positions that improper body movement have had to account for
3. Result of the proper swing sequence
4. Ability to use technique, creativity, vision on the golf course

Below I want you to comprise a list of local teaching professionals in your area. I want you to take some time to call them and discuss their philosophy, rates, and time availability. When you contact them, think about your learning style and if that teacher is right for you. Don't be set on PGA credentials. There are many good instructors who are not members of the PGA. **Don't be afraid to ask them for references.** You are about to entrust your golf future with this person and you want to make sure he/she is right for you.

Name   Phone # or email   rates

Now make a list of valuable golf websites that have simple, meaningful, golf advice and write down what 1-2 key swing thoughts you can take with you to the range and course.

SUCCESSFUL AND MEANINGFUL PRACTICE

THE COMPLETE GOLFER

PHASE 4: SUCCESSFUL AND MEANINGFUL PRACTICE
Mind prepared! Body Prepared! Let's take it to the range!

In this section you will learn about the following areas:
- Three types of practice (warm-up, maintenance, and preparation)
    - When is the best time to use them?
- Range warm-up drills
- Swing Drills for position, rhythm, feel
- Effective use of driving range practice time
- Easy to use teaching aids
- How to use the golf course for practice
- Fundamentals of the short game
- Effective use of short game practice time
    - Putting, chipping, pitching, wedges
    - I refer to this as the "SCORING ZONE"
- Repetitive and competitive practice drills and games

Section Reading Focus: Driving Range

- How do you currently practice?
- Do you feel that the quantity of balls hit is better than the quality of balls hit?
- Do you have a practice regimen or break down of how you use your range time?
  - Do you have an effective pre-game warm up?
  - Do you have a series of drills that you can use to get you back to a good feel of your golf swing?
- Do you know how to:
  - Make a swing change?
  - Maintain a current good swing?
- Do you have the right teaching/practice aids and drills to reinforce positive golf movements?
- Are you able to take your "Driving Range Swing" out to the course?

BE AT "HOME ON THE RANGE"

"Undirected practice is worse than no practice. Too often you become careless and sloppy in your swing. You'd be better off staying at home and beating rugs!"- Gary Player

"There aren't enough hours in the day to hit all the shots required in golf" – Ben Hogan

"The truth is in the dirt"- Ben Hogan

As I have stated before, you should incorporate "game situations" into your practice. Compete with yourself on the range and around the green. Set goals and have specific targets. Make the range into your golf course.

A book I recommend is *The Game before the Game* by Lynn Marriott and Pia Nilsson. They describe three types of practice:

1. *Warm-Up Practice*: This is the type of practice done prior to playing. Its purpose is to loosen the muscles and prepare for the course and competition. Swing changes and advanced swing thoughts should not occur here. The best method is to get tuned into the swing sensation you want to have in your round.

2. *Maintenance Practice:* This is done to maintain your current skills between rounds and to keep your game and swing performing efficiently. It could include very small changes to your swing that will not throw off the natural rhythm and balance needed during the height of your season.

3. *Preparation Practice:* This is about change or preparation for the future. It is about learning a new shot for a specific course. It includes a measurable swing change. This type of practice takes the most time to refine. I recommend this during the early season prior to competition or the late season after competition. Optimally, it is done during the off-season under the trained supervision of your teaching or club professional.

Range Warm-Up Drills

These drills are designed to loosen muscles and prepare the body for competition. They are designed to build confidence and establish a smooth tempo, rhythm, balance. I often have my students use tees when doing any type of drill work. These are also very good tempo drills to work on when you are swinging too fast (maintenance practice).

1. Shadow Swings: Slow motion full swings feeling the proper movement and sequence you want in the swing. Done without a ball.

2. 50 % swings: Full swings done at 50 % power from mid iron to driver. Make full swings at a teed ball but use your slower motion swing. If you hit your 7 iron 150 yards- this shot should only go 100 yards.
   a. This is the best rhythm drill I have ever used.

3. Feet together: use the big muscles of the upper body to establish connection, coil, and balance. If you can't hold your balance with your feet together, you are swinging too hard or your body dynamics are way out of synch.
   a. As you get loose, get the feet a little wider and then build into your full swing.
   b. This is another great drill to get your tempo and rhythm flowing
4. L to L: Swing to an L in the backswing (lead arm parallel to ground and 90 degree hinge) to an L on the follow through (trail arm parallel to ground with 90 degree unhinge). Make sure you are connected and turning throughout swing.
5. Triangle shots- Short shots focused on the keeping the triangle of the arms and shoulders connected. This would be about a half-swing to half-finish position.
   a. This is my second favorite drill as it keeps me connected and gives me a great impact position.
   b. You can tuck your sleeves into your arm pit to get the feeling of connection.
   c. You can place a tee in each armpit to get the feeling of connection.
6. Game shots- Play the course on the range. This incorporates using a variety of clubs and tee shots that you would be using on the course to be played.

Remember: When you are on the range, it is not the quantity of balls hit but the quality of balls hit that will provide you the greatest success. Always try to leave a few balls in the bucket!

Question: Do you use a practice station when you are on the driving range

- Alignment sticks
- Boards
- Swing plane sticks
- Mirror

- Launch monitor
- V1, Hudi (Ubersense)

Maintenance Drills that are designed to keep you playing well

1. These include practice stations and swing aids that reinforce what you are doing
   a. Alignment sticks should always be used on the range.
   b. There are a variety of swing plane tools that can keep your swing grooved or could be used in the Preparation/Change situation.
   c. These include rhythm drills and sensations that put you into the right positions and feelings.
   d. These drills reinforce and embed what has already been learned.
   e. Continue to go through your pre-shot routine and focus on specific targets.
   f. I feel the drills mentioned above are good drills for both warm up and maintenance

Preparation Drills- designed to help you learn something new; from a shot to an all-out swing change

1. These drills will take longer to implement and find comfort with.
2. They are designed to significantly alter a swing or mind set.
3. These shouldn't be done without correct supervision and instruction.
4. These would be done to fix the 7 common swing errors I mentioned earlier in this section.

Question: What category of practice do you use? Are you always working on something new? Do you feel your swing is in a good spot and needs repetition to maintain it?

My personal range session example: I realize that we don't all have the same amount of time to practice. Find the system that works best for you given the time you have. This would be more of a maintenance session for me. If I'm in preparation drill mode (swing change), I'll practice a drill for a considerable amount of time over days or weeks.

- 50% full motion swings off a tee with a 6 iron (5 minutes)
- Triangle swings with various clubs (15 minutes)
- 50-80 yard wedges (15 minutes)
- Full wedges (15 minutes)
- Short irons (15 minutes)
- Hybrid, 3 wood, Driver (15 minutes)
- Short Wedges (15 minutes)
- Short irons (15 minutes)

I may not always stick to this format. It is not set in stone. I may work longer on a problem area and shorter on another area if it feels good. I think it is important to note that the majority of my practice time is spent with scoring clubs- wedges and short irons. Too many times I see people grab the driver, hit a bucket, and walk off. That is not effective use of practice time to make yourself "A Complete Golfer".

How I would structure a lesson for a student:
- Discussion of strengths and weaknesses
  - What does the student do well with and struggle with?
- Discussion of goals and aspirations
  - What does the student want out of the lesson or series of lessons?
- Evaluation and Diagnosis
  - What do I see wrong with the swing?
  - What do I see right with the swing?
  - Physical body capabilities or inabilities
- Discussion of where we want to get to and how we want to do it
  - Devise a plan
- Lesson Process

- ○ Hit golf balls
- ○ Implement appropriate drills and reinforce those drills
- Lesson plan sheet
  - ○ Summary of what we did, what we want to do, and the drills needed to get the job done

TEACHING AIDS: Here is a list of my favorite teaching aids (and they are very cheap to acquire)

THE SWIMMING NOODLE: May be one of the best teaching devices on the market. For people who swing "over-the-top" or take it away too steep I place it on the outside of the ball. This teaches them to swing inside the noodle. Start with small swings and gradually build. For people who are too flat in their takeaway, I place it inside the ball plane and your goal is to not touch it on the backswing. Its natural curve is a great visual for swing path. You can cut one in half (length wise) and stand on it to improve balance.

BALL: Another great device is the use of a light medicine ball, volley ball or ball of equivalent size. I actually use a 9"rhino dodge ball. I have my students use this to get the feel of the triangle formed by the arms and shoulders and keeping the connection in the arm pits back and through the swing. This drill does a great job of creating turn while keeping the arms connected to the body (remember that connection is in the arm pits, not the arms connected to the sides of your body). This drill helps counteract excessive lift of the arms in the swing. The feeling is that there is a metal rod that goes through your shoulders and chest (or a belt tied around your shoulders) to prevent lift. We will spend time tossing the ball back and forth to get the proper feel of connection, load, and finish.

FLEXIBLE DRAINAGE PIPE: I use about 10" of flexible drainage pipe and place it up each arm. This helps create the feeling of width in the swing- although you can only take very short swings with it. It is also great for chipping and pitching practice.

ALIGNMENT STICKS: These can be used for alignment (one stick goes to your target line and the other parallel to your target line) or stuck in the ground at shaft angle for swing plane.

TENNIS OR BADMINTON RACKET: This can be used to visualize and teach the proper forearm/wrist rotation at impact.

WEIGHTED CLUB: This allows the feeling of swinging and releasing the club. Gravity allows the club to swing on the right path and the weight allows the proper hinge and forearm rotation. Many of these come with a "cheater grip" to get used to getting your hands on the club properly.

SWING FAN: Using this produces resistance in the swing which allows you to build the golf muscles and improve swing speed.

PORTABLE MIRROR (Uber 360- eyelinegolf.com)**:** This is a mirror you can place on the ground while hitting balls to look at positions during the swing.

IPAD/PHONE- Obviously there is some expense here. I use my IPAD with two apps; Ubersense and V1 swing video technology

There are many other drills I use to cure specific problems. If you are not in the position to take lessons, I suggest you look at the instructional sources I listed in the appendix. I'm a visual learner and get great information from my DVD's and internet sites (Michael Breed, Revolution Golf, Rotary Swing Golf) and I'm not embarrassed to say that I've learned a great deal from those sources and incorporate it into my teaching

ON COURSE PRACTICE

Reading Focus

- Do you always keep score in a round?
- Do you take a break from scoring a round to "practice" on the course?
- Do you use what you have done on the range and implement it on the course?
- Do you take time to practice various shots from hilly lies and areas around the green?

It is vital to PRACTICE on the course to be prepared for all the shots that you will hit in competition. When I was coaching, and even today with my golf students, I encouraged my players to go out alone in the evening and play a few holes but hit a variety of shots. The emphasis is not on score but on shot making and game situations. It is not uncommon for me to play 9 holes but get in 100+ game shots including drives, irons, wedges, chipping, pitching, putting, and bunkers. The range can't give you the multitude of lies and situations that the course can give you. As much as I love to hit balls, I know that is imperative for competition that I get "game shots" in as well. We all have to LEARN how to play golf. By practicing on the course you are focused on the process, not the result (score).

Game Practice Situations/Simulations

1. One person scramble
   a. A player hits a shot. If they don't like that shot, they can hit another and proceed from the best location. This is a great way to learn to "go-low."
   b. Alternative: A player hits a shot. He has the CHOICE to hit another shot but if he does hit another, he has to play it. This builds confidence and also incorporates a little pressure on the second shot.

    c. Worst shot- A player hits two shots. He has to play from the worst location. This teaches shot making, patience, and strategy.

2. Short game focus
   a. Purposely miss all the greens by hitting at a greenside target (bunker, back right, short left, short side, mound on the right, etc.) Practice from all the places you "missed" to.
   b. 100 yards and in: Take only your wedges and putter on the course and work on your distances with all the clubs. Ideally, your score from 100 and in should be less than 27 for 9 holes.
   c. 1,2, or 3 club tournament: Play the course with up to 3 clubs. This is a great activity for shot making, strategy, and creativity.
   d. Course Points Scorecard: See scorecard example in the "forms" section in appendix.
   e. Pars and Pennies: Start with 25 pennies in one pocket. For a positive result (birdie, fairway, green in regulation, up and in….), you move a penny (or two) to the opposite pocket. For a poor shot (bogey, drive in rough, 3 putt…), you replace a penny. The goal is to have more positive pennies than negative pennies. This is a great game as it brings immediate reinforcement. It brings competition between playing partners or teammates when they say "Ooooh, that'll cost you a penny!"
      - I did this with my high school teams and we had a challenge to see who had the most positive pennies at the end of the round.
      - You can eliminate the negative reinforcement by allowing them to move a penny on good shots and not moving a penny on negative shots.

3. Hit 'Til Your Happy: I prefer to practice in the evening or early in the morning on the course. This way I can drop a number of balls and hit shots. I never leave the spot until I'm satisfied

that I made the right swing and right shot. This is where I try to do the majority of my short game (chipping, pitching, putting, bunker) practice.

Question: How do you intend to incorporate purposeful practice while on the golf course? Which of the above methods work for you? Feel free to come up with a new on-course practice method.

Use this area to record any additional notes or main ideas that you want to stress.

CHIPPING AND PUTTING PRACTICE

"Approaching a putt with doubt in your mind is nearly always fatal" – Bobby Locke

Question: Do you approach a putt without a doubt in your mind that you will make it? I strongly believe that putting is 70% confidence and 30% mechanics; and I might be underestimating the confidence percent!

Reading Focus:

- Do you have a practice putting routine?
- Do you have any practice aids? (putting arc, mirror, metronome, etc)
- Do you go through your actual putting routine while practicing to reinforce what you want to do on the course (mark, line up, practice strokes)?
- Do you practice your short putts (kill zone) and your lag putting along with sloping and speed putts?
- Do you approach a putt knowing you are going to make it; that all of your hard work and preparation will pay off?
- Do you let a missed putt affect the next shot or the next putt?
- Do you incorporate internal competition when you practice putting?
- What percentage of time do you spend practicing your short game(wedges and putter)? It should comprise 50-60% of all practice time!

Focus on the quality of time put in rather than the quantity of shots hit and be cautious not to make this portion of your practice routine too monotonous. Make sure you vary the types of short shots you are hitting and the targets you are hitting to. In short game practice (pitching, chipping, putting, and bunkers) you need to have some routine drill work but also incorporate trouble shots and creativity.

The best short-game artists have tremendous vision and feel for the shot they are going to hit.

Putting Strategies: How to become a better putter NOW!

1. The most important thing in gaining confidence in putting is to practice MAKING putts. Start off with 25, 50, even 100 putts inside 3 feet. Players need to see and hear the ball going in the hole.
2. Four factors of putting: line, pace, balance, stillness (of body and mind).
3. Don't practice putts that have a greater chance of missing than making.
    a. For lag/speed putting- practice from fringe to fringe or spot to spot.
    b. Don't practice missing putts. Gain confidence by making short putts.
4. Which is more important: Distance or Direction? Most teachers and players feel that distance is much more important than direction.
    *   Work on finding the right length of stroke for 10, 15, 20, 30 foot putts.
5. Most of the idea of "making" putts should be from 15 feet and in. If you become a solid putter from 15 feet and in and work on distance putting, your scores will lower significantly.
    a. You will reduce 3 putting by a large margin by lag (or distance) putting to an area and being able to hole the 3-5 footers with regularity.
6. Confidence is crucial to good putting. Again, the more putts you make in practice, the more routine those putts will become.
    a. Develop your putting mantra: "I am a great putter from 5 feet and in".
7. Develop a consistent and methodical routine that incorporates breathing, visualization, and positive thoughts.
    a. Have a quiet mind over your putts.

     b. See the ball following the intended line and going in.

     c. Try to do the same routine (visualize, aim, practice strokes, self-talk) over every putt

8. At the end of this manual there are some practice sheets you can use to focus in on where you need to work and/or how to establish a consistent putting practice.

Putting Fundamentals (STILL MIND; STILL BODY)

Note: putting is a very individual thing. Like the golf swing, there is no "One size fits all" putting method. What's important is that you develop a consistent stroke with decent fundamentals and truly believe you are a great putter.

There are many putting variations to choose from. Described below are the basics of good standard putting. When using the "claw", "pencil", "saw", or reverse putting grip…. A belly or chest putter, there are other things that are brought into play. When standard putting is no longer an option for you there are other alternatives. Most of them are to reduce the "wiggle or twitch" factor of the hands in your putting stroke.

I am an advocate of using less speed and playing more break. The idea here is to die the ball in the hole. That way you can use the entire circumference of the hole. I'm also an advocate of using a thicker putter grip to get it more securely in the palms of your hands (Super-stroke; jumbo).

1. Make sure the putter is cut to the right length for you and matches your putting stroke and style.

2. There are a number of putter lengths and grips out there. Find the one that gives you the best stroke and ability to make the most putts.

3. The putter grip should be more in the palms (lifeline) of both hands. Both palms face each other and the thumbs go down the shaft.

4. Posture:
    - Bend at hips with knees slightly flexed.
    - Arms hang comfortably from shoulder sockets and elbows close to body.
    - Keep in mind the "Triangle" formed by the arms and shoulders in your set up.
        o A good putting stroke is as simple as rocking the triangle back and forth.
    - Weight is about 50/50 or favors the "hole-side" foot.
    - The triangle is one thought…
        o Another good image is a "Y" formed by the arms, shoulders and putter shaft.
        o You want to keep that "Y" constant throughout your stroke.
5. Keep the putter low to the ground through your putting stroke.
    - Determine if you are an arc putter or square to square putter.
    - Both are perfectly acceptable but common teaching today tends to go with the arc method (research Stan Utley on this).
        o Square to square- putter goes straight back and through; shoulders rock.
        o Arc- the putter naturally curves with the arc created by the turn of the chest and shoulders; there is more of a release of the putter head in this method.
    - Regardless of arc or square method, the putting stroke should not be manipulated with the hands but should have a big muscle feel (shoulders and arms).
    - There are a number of putting arcs on the market to help build the repetition needed (eyelinegolf.com).
    - For a square-to square-method: Place your alignment sticks on the ground at the width of your putter and putt between them.

- Another good putting aid is placing the ball between two tees the width of your putter and practice making putts without hitting the tees.

6. Eyes and body remain on the same plane and in the same posture. Head stays steady and eyes remain fixed on the ball.
    - COMMON MISTAKE: The body loses its posture on the follow through as the head lifts or moves forward and the putter comes high off the ground.
    - COMMON MISTAKE: Knees and hips move- losing the natural square or arc method
    - A putting mirror can help self-check these (eyelinegolf.com).

7. Consistent pace, rhythm, tempo, and length of stroke in putting (and chipping) is vital.
    - Avoid a "hit" or "jab" in the putting stroke- leads to inconsistency.
    - COMMON MISTAKE: Deceleration- When the putter moves slowly, even quits or recoils at impact. Make sure the right amount of energy is being delivered at impact (without a jab or hit!).
    - TRY TO MATCH THE LENGTH OF YOUR BACK STROKE TO THE THROUGH STROKE, developing a consistent rhythm and pace of your stroke.
    - In putting and chipping it is imperative to keep wrist angle fixed.

8. Remember: We all miss putts. It's not the end of the world. Our goal is to improve our confidence, process, practice and routine so that we increase our chances of making more putts.

9. NEVER let the putter head pass the hands on the follow through. Maintain the wrist angle set at address through the stroke.

Short Putting Drills and Training Aids- I highly recommend a guide/aim line on every ball. It helps in alignment and examining roll characteristics of the ball coming off the putter head.

Note: My two favorite putting devices to purchase would be a putting arc and putting mirror. Both of these can be found in golf stores and online (www.eyelinegolf.com). Another useful device is an alignment rod placed on the outside of the ball. Make putts without letting the putter cross over the alignment rod.

1. Around the world: Place 6-8 tees around the hole about 3 feet away. Putt a ball from each spot. If you miss one, start over. Complete 3-5 times in a row. Reinforces competition feel and short putts with different break.

2. Tee Ball: Put two tees the width of a putter head 3-5 feet from the hole on all four sides of the hole. Place the ball in the middle of the tees. The goal is to stroke the putt without hitting the tees. This provides immediate feedback on stroke path and various breaks around the hole.

3. The Putting Board (Arc putting)
   - If you can't afford a putting arc, you can rip a 4x4 to a 60 degree angle. Place the ball off the angled edge and hit putts keeping the putter along the edge to feel the right path.
   - I've also used the straight side of a board as well. Place the ball on the inside of the straight side and practice putts not hitting the board back or through. The natural putting movement should produce a slight arc that gets a little closer to your trail foot in the backstroke and a little closer to your lead foot in the through stroke.
     - NOTE- the putter should never get farther from your feet in your stroke- either parallel to square foot line or a bit of an arc.
   - You may want to put a couple of nails in the board to hold it in place.

4. Parallel Sticks or Shafts (square to square) : Use two parallel clubs or alignment sticks on the ground facing your target. Line them up just outside your putter head. Place the ball in the middle and practice making putts keeping the putter between the sticks.

- A variation is to use two dozen ball boxes or two thick phone books in the same method. This gives the drill some height and better feedback if you lift your putter off line.

5. String Drill: Use two golf pencils with a 5-10 foot piece of string attached to the top of them. Put one pencil in the ground behind the hole (or to the side of the hold depending on break) and one pencil back so the string is tight. Put the ball under the string and make putts keeping your putter under the string.

   - The putter can go straight back and through or arc a little depending on your stroke
   - The putter should never go "outside" of the string (farther from your foot line).
   - Variation/Extension for breaking putts- place a third string on the line of the apex of your putt. This will help you to see that every putt should be approached as straight- a straight putt to the apex of your breaking putt.

6. Yardstick: Put a ball at the end of a yardstick. Putt the ball off the yardstick using the stick as a guide. Make sure the putter "scrapes" the yardstick for a few inches back and through.

My goal for you: Develop 2-3 drills or putting aids that you can use to create a positive thought over every putt.

Question: Which of the above putting drills work for you?

Lag Putting/ Distance Drills and games: I recommend not even putting to a hole for these- Remember: we don't want to practice missing putts! The key is to control distance, not necessarily make the putt.

1. *Fringe to Fringe*: Putt across the green from fringe to fringe getting it as close to the fringe as possible without hitting

the fringe. Tees could be placed 12-17" from the fringe in a box shape and try to lag the putts into the box.

2. *Four tee drill (my favorite)*: Place a tee at 20, 30, and 40 feet from an area that is marked off by 4 tees about 3 feet by 3 feet (or larger if you want). From each distance practice getting the ball into the box of tees. This is a good drill because you learn the amount of stroke you need for those distances.
   • You can make a competition or game out of this.
   • You can also place 6 tees around the hole with the first two tees about 3 feet short of the hole. The second two tees equal to the hole and place the last two 2 tees 3 feet behind the hole. You get 1 point for getting it into the short box, 2 points for getting it in the back box, and 3 points for making the putt.
3. *Eyes closed*: Great way to get the feel of distance putts.
4. *Step ladder*: Putt to a tee 10 feet away, then 15 feet, then 20 feet and so on….
5. *Step ladder variation*: Putt one ball, then double the distance on the next putt, then double that distance…..
6. *21*: Pick two holes at least 20 feet from one another. Using one ball against your opponent, putt to the hole. The person who is closest gets one point. If you lip the cup you get two points (if you are still closest) and if you make the putt you get three points. You have to get 21 points. If you are at 19 points and you make the putt…. You go back to zero.
7. *Horse*: Against a partner, pick a hole to putt to. If you make the putt, the opponent has to make the putt or they get a letter. First with 5 letters or points, loses
   • Since this game focuses on making putts, the putts shouldn't be over 10 feet

I said you would become a better putter NOW! Which of these games and drills do you find the most beneficial and fun to practice your putting and incorporate some internal competition?

Chipping Fundamentals

Reading Focus:
- Do you have a routine for chipping?
- Do you practice a variety of lies with different clubs?
- Do you have a feel and vision for the type of short shot you want to play?
  - Fundamentals are important but you still need to be creative with your short game shots.
- Do you incorporate internal competition while practicing?

Basic Guideposts of Chipping and Pitching

1. Good posture and remain in your posture through chip or pitch.
2. Start left, stay left (right handed golfer): This means the weight should be on the "hole-side" foot and stay there throughout the chip shot.
   a. Have crisp, downward contact. Don't fall back or try to "help" the ball into the air
   b. Rule: Hit down to make the ball go up!
3. Try to match the distance of the backswing and through swing to get good rhythm and tempo.
4. The handle should always lead the club head for crisp contact.
5. Lean towards the target- weight on hole-side foot and keep it there through the shot to ensure crisp contact. Don't try to help the ball in the air!
   - You may also want to feel like your nose is ahead of the ball at address.
   - DON'T LET YOUR SPINE AND WEIGHT SHIFT AWAY FROM THE HOLE THROUGH THE SHOT.
6. Top hand wrist should stay flat through impact for a basic chip or pitch.

7. Head and body stay centered over the ball or slightly ahead-producing crisp contact- weight stays on front foot through shot
8. Club stays low to ground and body (arms, chest,hips) move the club through
9. Ball should be behind the center of your stance
10. Generally speaking…
    *   Get the ball rolling on the green as soon as possible
    *   The more green you have to work with the more you want to run it (less lofted club)
    *   The less green you have to work with the more you want to fly it (more lofted club)
11. Visualize an area or spot you want the ball to land.
12. My general rule depending on green speed: Land a chip 1/3 of the way in the air. Land a pitch shot about 1/2 of the way in the air and a flop shot 3/4 of the way in the air
    *   You can put a towel on the green as a guide to land the ball over to simulate a bunker or long fringe area.
13. Triangle chipping and pitching- This method utilizes stable arms and wrists. Turn the triangle (chest and arms together) back and through with no hinging of wrists. This is a rotational movement of the upper body (Steve Stricker).
14. Hinge and hold: Slight pivot or turn in the backswing with a little wrist hinge. Hold that hinge through impact (don't let wrists unhinge) and make sure you turn back through the ball.
15. Practice from a variety of lies and incorporate creativity as well as technique in your practice.

Chipping and Pitching drills and games

1. *The Bench* (from Harvey Penick): Pull a bench over to the green. You can practice a chip and run by hitting the shot under the bench and a pitch or flop by hitting it over the bench. The crash of the ball against the bench provides the necessary reinforcement if you are not doing it correctly!

2. *Back Heel Up*: If you find yourself hitting thin or fat chips, practice with your back heel up. This forces you to keep your weight on your front foot. You could also "shift or point" your back knee more towards the target to stabilize lower body.

3. *Two Club Chips*: Hold a club in regular chipping position, then hold another club as an extension of the shaft off your front hip. That extension should not change direction or "hit" your front hip through impact.

   - Better method- You may also use a thin metal rod placed in the hole in the end of your grip to accomplish this so you are not holding two clubs to chip with.

4. Chipping boards (or phone books): Set up two boards or barriers to chip through to fix the path of your stroke (similar to above putting drill).

5. When working on technique, it is ok to hit 20 or 30 chips or pitches in a row. I recommend you keep a "practice" bag of balls that are similar to the balls you use in normal play.

6. Competition and games: Try to incorporate pressure and competition into your practice. These are not technique games. They are designed to invoke a form of competition and pressure into your practice. They should be done at the end of each of your short game practice sessions.

   a. *Pick-A-Shot*: 2 or more golfers- A person picks a club and shot. Everyone has to hit that club. The person who is closest to the pin gets the point and gets to pick the next club and shot.

   b. *Nine*: Pick 5 balls and chip or pitch to a hole. Hit the five shots then go putt them in. Par is 10. Your goal is to get 9 by making one of the chips. This is a combination game that utilizes chipping or pitching and putting. Stay there until you get 9!

      - Mike Small (Coach- University of Illinois) requires his players to do a chipping drill until they chip in 5 in a row from a specific spot before they can move on or quit for the day.

    c. *Up and In*: Use one ball and hit a chip or pitch. Then go and putt the ball in. Move around the green to various lies, distances, and wedges.

More Related to Pitching/flop shots

1. The biggest goal here is to determine the length of swing needed and degree of loft on the ball needed to get the ball in the correct area and stop in the right distance.
2. The higher you want the ball to go the lower you set your hands at address. Increase your distance from the ball a couple of inches. Stabilize your lower body and feel like you are hitting the shot with core rotation and connection. To hit the ball even higher add a certain amount of wrist hinge.
3. Other Pitching Drills:
   - *Laundry baskets*: Place a number of smaller laundry baskets on or around the green or out on the practice tee at distances of 10, 20, 30 feet and try to land balls in the baskets. You could use any variety of markers or plates.
     - I also do this on the range at 20,30,40…. 100 yards to work on a variety of wedge distances
   - *Towel Drill*: Place a towel 8-12" short of where you want the ball to land. Anything short of the towel simulates a bunker or hazard
   - *Ladder Drill*: Hit a wedge to 20 yards, then to 30 yards, then to 40 yards and so forth. At the end of that maximum distance of that club, go backwards to the shortest distance then go back out to the maximum distance
   - *Feet Together*: Hit short pitch shots with your feet together to get the feeling of upper body rotation-reducing instability caused by hips and legs.
     - Distance in short shots should be controlled/ created through rotational speed of chest, arms,

shoulders through impact… NOT by hands, hips, legs, and feet

Overall Practice Summary:

My favorite range warm up drill is:

My favorite range practice drill is:

What I found when I had a committed and meaningful practice session was:

When I develop an effective practice routine I was able to:

My favorite putting drill or thought is:

My Favorite chipping/pitching drill is:

I found that when I incorporated some internal competition during practice I was able to:

TAKING IT TO THE COURSE

THE COMPLETE GOLFER

PHASE 5: TAKING IT TO THE COURSE
Taking mental prep, body prep, practice prep to the Golf Course!

In this final section we will discuss how to take what you have learned to the golf course.
- **What to focus on while playing golf**
- **How to react to your shots**
- **How to break out of your comfort zone**
- **How to score lower**

If you have dedicated yourself to phases 1-4 of becoming a complete golfer, you should have what you need to make the leap to the golf course. I assume you have not banished yourself from golf while reading this manual. I assume you have taken some of what you have read and put it into practice. Golf is a process of trial and error. It is a process or journey of mental preparation, physical preparation, practice and performance.

A round of golf:

Warm-up and preparation

- Warm up drills that work for you and put you in a positive state of mind.
- Visualize the course you are going to play as you warm up and hit shots on the range that you plan on hitting on the course.
    - Eliminate the surprise factor as much as possible.
- Find places on the putting green to practice from to give you a feel for the greens and flag positions on the course.
- Identify the flight and trajectory that you are most comfortable with that day.
- Practice your pre-shot routine.
- Devise your strategy for playing the course.
- A WARM-UP SESSION IS NO PLACE TO MAKE MAJOR SWING CHANGES!

Playing the Game

- REMEMBER- THIS IS A GAME. IT IS MEANT TO BE FUN AND ENJOYABLE.
- Enjoy your surroundings and the people you are with.
- Stick to your routine to provide balance, organization, and breathing.
- Pick out specific targets and take dead aim.

- Stick to your game plan for that day.
  - If you spent time preparing a game plan for the course, then that is what your body is ready for; don't switch it up- that may produce more stress.
- Approach each shot with a positive thought and mantra.
  - Talk yourself into hitting good shots.
- Don't put too much emphasis on a bad shot; it will stick with you on the next shot.
- If you hit a poor shot, remember it doesn't define who you are. It was a mistake. Mistakes happen. Go through your post-shot simulation to get the right feel for the next shot. LET IT GO!
- Don't let a bad shot lead to another bad shot. LET IT GO!
- Congratulate yourself on a good shot and move on.
- Keep track of your statistics to analyze what you did well and what you need to improve.
- Be thankful you had the opportunity to play. There are millions of people in the world who will never hold a golf club, enjoy the time with friends and family, or see the natural scenery that golf affords us.

Best of luck in your journey to becoming a "Complete Golfer".

Paul Meyer

The Golfing Guy

A BRIEF SIDEBAR FOR PARENTS AND COACHES

The golf coach's job has been redefined in recent years. Time was that the coaches could play during competition. Thankfully that has changed and the coach has more responsibility to monitor play, make rulings, and support their players during competition. But, is every coach ready to do those things? I always felt my job was to be on the course-coaching. It is important for coaches to have an understanding of what should and shouldn't be done while a player is playing. That goes for parents as well. I didn't change swings on the course. I let them bounce ideas off me and discuss strategy. I was confined by the "green-to-tee" rule. I could only contact players from green to tee and not during the play of the hole. That has also changed (and for the better) to continued contact through the round between player and coach. I still think that time should be used to keep players positive and focused and to calm down their nerves and help let off steam. A good coach is a sounding board as well as teacher.

Whether it is a parent, coach, or spectator the most important job they have on the course is to give encouragement to the player. I've seen many golf coaches and parents give the head-shake or deep sigh of anguish and exasperation towards a player. Players feed off that energy. Golf must be played from the positive side and the people around that player must react accordingly. You have to establish a relationship with your players or child so they are willing to accept you on the course and they know so when they talk to you or see you, you are ready with positive reinforcement to keep them going or get them back on track. You are their only ally on that golf course and they have to know you are there for them to lean on.

Parents have a huge impact on their kids. Golfers will feed off the energy around them. Parents and coaches shaking their head in frustration, disgust, or disappointment will only make things worse. It is not much better for the parents and coaches to grill their player after a round; going through analytical dissection of each and every second of the event. Sure, I think it is important for some post-game discussion and analysis, but there is a good way and bad way to do it. The constant rehashing of what went bad during the round will reinforce negative thoughts and lead to a relationship issue between the kid and adult. Kids have to realize they are playing for themselves first, their team/school second, and nobody else after that. Golfers and athletes can't play for other people. It is way too much pressure for a young athlete to handle. They need to focus on their job of playing golf to the best of their ability that day.

You don't need to be a golf professional to offer praise, support, and encouragement on the golf course. With more and more coaches and parents on the course and at competitions, the expectations are changing. Coaches need to be aware of things they can do on the course that will help a player get through the mental, emotional, strategic, and physical challenges of the match or tournament they are playing in.

That being said, I do think that it is important that each player conducts him/herself appropriately on the golf course. All golfers need to observe course etiquette, good sportsmanship and play by the rules of golf and competition. If negative behavior is exhibited, the coach and parent have every right and duty to re-teach that player what is acceptable and unacceptable behavior on the course. I can even say that I was "benched" one match in high school for not following team rules. It happens to all of us. The important thing is to learn from our mistakes-whether they are on the golf course or in life. Learning from our mistakes is what makes us better people.

APPENDIX

- Use the forms in this section to set up your personalized practice sessions
- You will find lists of my suggestions for other reading material, media, internet sites that can benefit you in your golf journey

STRATEGY AND COURSE MANAGEMENT SELF-ASSESSMENT

Player: _____   Date: _____

Please rank your current level of proficiency in course management in the following areas (5 being excellent, 1 being poor or non-existent)

Pre-shot Routine

1.	I have a pre-shot routine that is the same for every shot	1	2	3	4	5
2.	I stick to my routine no matter the circumstances	1	2	3	4	5
	· Plan to improve:					

Relaxation, trust, focus

1.	I use breathing techniques to relax mind and body	1	2	3	4	5
2.	I use positive self-talk or a mantra before each shot	1	2	3	4	5
3.	I have a clear picture of the shot I want to hit	1	2	3	4	5
4.	I trust my decision and commit to the shot	1	2	3	4	5
5.	I accept the outcome and move on to the next shot	1	2	3	4	5
6.	I play in the present (not affected by past shots or thinking about future shots)	1	2	3	4	5
7.	I am focused on my target (not on hazards or trouble)	1	2	3	4	5
8.	I practice with a purpose (quality, plan, specific goal)	1	2	3	4	5
9.	I approach each course with a game plan and stick to it	1	2	3	4	5
10.	I play what the course gives me and adjust my game plan accordingly	1	2	3	4	5
	• Plan to improve:					

Trouble shots (ability to hit the following)

•	Low fade	1	2	3	4	5
•	High fade	1	2	3	4	5
•	Low draw	1	2	3	4	5
•	High draw	1	2	3	4	5
•	¾ wind shot/ low punch	1	2	3	4	5
•	Plan to improve:					

SHORT GAME/GREENSIDE PRACTICE SHEET

(Do this every few weeks to chart progress)

Player: _____   Date: _____

Short Putts

·   4 tees around the hole at 3 feet X 10   _____/40

·   4 tees around the hole at 5 feet X 10   _____/40

·   2 tees opposite side of hole at 10 feet X 2   _____/20

Lag Putts

·   20 feet into a 4 X 4' box (4 tees) X 20   _____/20

·   30 feet into a 4 X 4' box (4 tees) X 20   _____/20

·   40 feet into a 5 X 5' box (4 tees) X 20   _____/20

Chipping

·   chips under a bench from fringe to a pin   _____/20
       about 25 feet to within 5 feet

·   Pitches/flops over a bench from rough   _____/20
       to pin about 15 feet on green

Combination Practice- see chipping and pitching games section

Up and In

·   Hit 1 chip/pitch and putt it X 10 (or more)   _____/10

·   Record how many you got up and in on out of 10

Nine

·   Chip/pitch 5 balls and putt them in   _____/ 5

·   Record how many times you got a score of 10 or better

Self Assessment:

My greatest strength in this practice was:

My greatest weakness in this practice was:

Plan for Improvement:

GOLF ROUND TOTAL GAME ANALYSIS

Use this scorecard to assess your complete golf round and track your progress

Hole:	1	2	3	4	5	6	7	8	9
Score:									
Fairway hit:									
GIR:									
Putts:									
Points:									
Hole:	10	11	12	13	14	15	16	17	18
Score:									
Fairway hit:									
GIR:									
Putts:									
Points:									

Point allocations:

Fairway :	+1
GIR:	+1
1 putt :	+1
Sand Save:	+1
Hole out:	+1
Par:	+1
Birdie:	+2
Eagle:	+4

Note: You can add your own positive points in here as well

Note: You may also subtract points: -1 for a 3-putt; -1 for a bogey; -1 for a penalty shot. Feel free to amend this scorecard to suit your needs

CUMULATIVE STAT SUMMARY SHEET

Use after a series of Total Game Analysis scorecards have been completed

Player:_____ Date(s):_____

Record 9 hole scores: _____, _____, _____, _____, _____, _____

Record 18 hole scores: _____, _____, _____, _____, _____, _____

9 Hole stroke average _____ (total strokes divided by number of rounds)

18 hole stroke average _____ (total strokes divided by number of rounds)

Fairways hit: _____ out of total possible fairways _____ = _____ %

Greens in Regulation hit: _____ out of total possible GIR _____ = _____ %

Total putts _____ divided by # of rounds _____ = _____ average putts per round

Greatest area of weakness:

Greatest strength:

Goal:

How to accomplish goal:

PRACTICE PLAN FOR TOTAL SCORING ZONE

**A comprehensive analysis of your putting and wedges
to be used after your short game practice session**

Player: _____   Date: _____

Short putts (10 feet and in- "The Kill Zone")   1 2 3 4 5

- Goal - 5/5 within 5 feet
- Goal- 3/5 from 10 feet
- Plan to improve:

Medium Putts (10-20 feet)   1 2 3 4 5

- Goal- all two putts or less
- Goal- make at least 4
- Plan to improve:

Lag Putts (20 + feet)   1 2 3 4 5

- Goal- all two putts or less
- Goal- occasional make
- Plan to improve:

Chipping (chip and run; green to work with)   1 2 3 4 5

- Goal- "Up and In" 70 % of attempts
- Goal- "Nine" completed in 5 attempts or less
- Plan to improve:

Pitching (flop, pitch; less green to work with or over hazard simulation) 1 2 3 4 5

- Goal- "Up and In" 70 % of attempts
- Goal- "Nine" completed in 5 attempts or less
- Plan to improve:

30 yard shots   1 2 3 4 5

- Goal- all on green within 15 feet of pin
- Up and in 60% of the time
- Plan to improve:

60 yard shots   1 2 3 4 5

- All within 15- 20 feet of pin and on green
- Up and In 40-50 % of time
- Plan to improve:

90 yard shots   1 2 3 4 5
- All within 20 feet of pin and on green
- Up and In 30-40 % of time

Recommended Books on Mental Golf

My best advice is to highlight, underline, or take
margin notes for easier reference and re-reading
Fearless Golf by Gio Valiente
The Ten Commandments of Mindpower Golf by Robert Winters
The Golfer's Mind and Golf is Not a Game of Perfect by Bob Rotella
Zen Golf and Zen Putting by Joseph Parent
Every Shot Must Have a Purpose by Pia Nilsson and Lynn Marriot
The Little Red Book (and others) by Harvey Penick
How I Play Golf by Tiger Woods
Your 15th Club: The Inner Secret to Great Golf by Bob Rotella
The Game Before the Game by Nilsson and Marriot
*Golf for Enlightenment: The Seven Lessons for
the Game of Life* by Deepak Chopra
Spirit of Golf by Tim Kremer
Wired to Win by David Breslow
Mastering Golf's Mental Game by Dr. Michael T. Lardon
Note: many of these are available in audio versions as well

PHYSICAL CONDITIONING RESOURCES

My top workout sources for total body conditioning: There are hundreds to choose from. I have these in my collection and have liked them or they have been recommended to me by others.

Jackie Warner DVD's

Jillian Michael's DVD's (Workout, Yoga Inferno, Yoga Meltdown)

P90X and Insanity

Katherine Robert's Yoga for Golfers DVD's

Beach Body Workouts

Medicine Ball and Kettlebell Workouts

Titleist Performance Institute (on line/DVD)

Resources I recommend for Instructional Concepts:

Internet: There is a whole world of "golf stuff" on the internet. Choose your sites carefully since anyone can post something on You tube.

- Revolution Golf is a great site!
- Golf Channel.Com/ Academy- join and get all their instructional video- especially the Golf Fix with Michael Breed
- Rotaryswinggolf.com
- Medicus 5SK methodology

Media and Book-

- *The 8 Step Swing* by Jim McLean (DVD)
- *Hogan Revealed* by Jim McLean (DVD)
- *Building Block Approach* by Jim McLean (DVD)
- *Golf's Energy Forces and Swing Motion* by Rick Bradshaw (DVD)

- The Golf Channel Academy series by Rick Smith and Jim McLean(DVD)
- *Butch Harmon About Golf* (DVD)
- *Golf Magazine's Guides to Playing Golf* (book series)
- *How I Play Golf* by Tiger Woods (Book)
- *Ben Hogan's Five Lessons* (Book)
- *Power Golf* by Ben Hogan (Book)
- *Golf My Way by Jack Nicklaus* (Book)
- *How to Build a Classic Swing* by Ernie Els (Book)
- *The Golfing Machine* by Homer Kelly (book)
- *On Learning Golf: A Valuable guide to Better Golf* by Percy Boomer (Book)

TEN MENTAL KEYS FOR PLAYING TOURNAMENT GOLF
R.K. Winters

"There are two kinds of golf: golf and tournament golf... and they are not at all the same."

Bobby Jones

1. Great golf begins with a great attitude
2. Believe in your ability and your talent
3. Play your own game
4. Play one shot at a time
5. Play with patience
6. Commit yourself to the moment
7. Keep things simple
8. Let go of expectations
9. Trust your thoughts and decisions
10. Never, ever give up

I often refer to the "First Tee's" Nine core values in my seminars and lessons. I think they spell out very simply how we should act on the golf course and in life. Those values are listed below. If you are a parent or coach I encourage you to get kids involved in the First Tee program in your area.

Nine Core Values

The First Tee has established Nine Core Values that represent some of the many inherently positive values connected with the game of golf. These Nine Core Values have been incorporated into The First Tee Experience and have been used to name golf holes at several of The First Tee facilities.

Honesty

The quality or state of being truthful; not deceptive

Golf is unique from other sports in that players regularly call penalties on themselves and report their own score.

Integrity

Strict adherence to a standard of value or conduct; personal honesty and independence

Golf is a game of etiquette and composure. Players are responsible for their actions and personal conduct on the golf course even at times when others may not be looking.

Sportsmanship

Observing the rules of play and winning or losing with grace

Players must know and abide by the rules of golf and be able to conduct themselves in a kind and respectful manner towards others even in a competitive game.

Respect

To feel or show deferential regard for; esteem

In golf it is important to show respect for oneself, playing partners, fellow competitors, the golf course, and for the honor and traditions of the game.

Confidence

Reliance or trust. A feeling of self-assurance

Confidence plays a key role in the level of play that one achieves. Players can increase confidence in their abilities by being positive and focusing on something they are doing well regardless of the outcome.

Responsibility

Accounting for one's actions; dependable

Players are responsible for their actions on the golf course. It is up to them to keep score, repair divots, rake bunkers, repair ball marks on the green, and keep up with the pace of play.

Perseverance

To persist in an idea, purpose or task despite obstacles

To succeed in golf, players must continue through bad breaks and their own mistakes, while learning from past experiences.

Courtesy

Considerate behavior toward others; a polite remark or gesture

A round of golf should begin and end with a handshake between fellow competitors. Players also should be still and quiet while others are preparing and performing a shot.

Judgment

The ability to make a decision or form an opinion; a decision reached after consideration

Using good judgment is very important in golf. It comes into play when deciding on strategy, club selection, when to play safe and when to take a chance, the type of shot players consider executing, as well as making healthy choices on and off the golf course.

CONTACT INFORMATION

For individual or group lessons, consultations, or seminars
for businesses or teams contact: Paul Meyer

Tampa, FL

thegolfingguy@msn.com

Paul Meyer: linkedin

Printed in the United States
By Bookmasters